Guerrilla Marketing With Technology

Guerrilla Marketing With Technology

Unleashing the Full Potential
of Your Small Business

Jay Conrad Levinson

Addison-Wesley
Reading, Massachusetts

Many of the designations used by manufacturers and sellers to distinguish their products are claimed as trademarks. Where those designations appear in this book and Addison-Wesley was aware of a trademark claim, the designations have been printed in initial capital letters.

Library of Congress Cataloging-in-Publication Data

Levinson, Jay Conrad.
   Guerrilla marketing with technology : unleashing the full potential of your small business / Jay Conrad Levinson
     p. cm.
   Includes index.
   ISBN 0-201-32804-6 (alk. paper)
   1. Marketing. 2. Small business—Management. 3. Internet marketing.
   HF5415.L4792   1997
   658.8—dc21   97-26619
                                        CIP

Addison-Wesley is an imprint of Addison Wesley Longman, Inc.

Cover design by Andrew Newman
Text design and production by Corsey & Linstromberg
Set in 10-point Cheltenham

123456789-MA-0100999897
First printing, September 1997

Addison-Wesley books are available at special discounts for bulk purchases in the U.S. by corporations, institutions, and other organizations. For more information, please contact the Corporate, Government, and Special Sales Department at Addison Wesley Longman, Inc., One Jacob Way, Reading, MA 01867, or call 1-800-238-9682.

Find us on the World Wide Web at
http://www.aw.com/gb/

Contents

Preface . . . **vii**

Acknowledgments . . . **ix**

1 / The Unfair Advantage . . . **1**

2 / The Virtual Guerrilla . . . **15**

3 / Marketing Your Small Business . . . **29**

4 / The Business of Customers . . . **43**

5 / Zero to 60 in 30 Days . . . **59**

6 / Saving Money by Saving Time . . . **71**

7 / The Benefits of Collaboration . . . **87**

8 / Mining the Treasures of the Internet . . . **101**

9 / High-Tech/High-Return Marketing . . . **119**

10 / The Glowing Future for Small Business . . . **135**

Glossary of Key Terms . . . **149**

Resources . . . **155**

Step-by-Step Start-Up Guides:

How to Select or
Upgrade a Personal Computer . . . **157**

How to Save Money by
Sharing Files, Printers, and More . . . **163**

How to Create and Deliver a Newsletter . . . **167**

How to Create Brochures and Flyers . . . **173**

How to Conduct Business
Research on the Internet . . . **177**

How to Create a Simple Web Page . . . **181**

55 Technology Tips . . . **187**

What's Your Techficiency Quotient? . . . **199**

Index . . . **205**

Preface

My first books were about making it as an entrepreneur. Then I began writing books about marketing. In between producing that multitude of marketing tomes, I've taken detours to write about San Francisco, time, photovoltaics, satellite television, and the Internet. Now it turns out I've written a book about technology.

I've never been much for technology. My wife is the one who programs the VCR. So am I writing about technology because I've changed a lot? Not really. I'm writing about technology because the world has changed a lot. It has become a lot more technological.

It's no longer possible to avoid advanced technology if you drive a car, make a phone call, microwave a meal, watch the tube, or travel by airplane. Last week I adjusted my satellite dish to pick up a new satellite, and although the task was a bit complex, I consoled myself by thinking that at least it wasn't rocket science—until I realized that it was rocket science and that it was happening in my own bedroom!

This book is for small business guerrillas who have noticed that technology is out there and that it just might propel them to their goals at rocket speed. Although that has probably been true for a long time, it is only very recently that even nontechnical types have been able to use technology.

Airplanes were around a long time before people were able to use them as part of normal life. Zippers were here for 40 years before people understood what they could do.

I've written this book because technology has come of age and is now within anyone's grasp. It is easier, more affordable, and more empowering than ever. Every guerrilla small business owner will be drawn to technology because it makes everything in business easier, and frees up more of their time for things unrelated to business.

As impersonal as you may have thought technology was, you'll see that just the opposite is true: it opens the door to warm and lasting human relationships; it makes connecting with people easier than ever; it grants you more of your most precious resource—time.

If you were in a rowboat drifting across the ocean and somebody offered you a set of oars to speed you on your way and keep you on your course, you'd never ignore the offer. Technology is your set of oars and until you take technology firmly into your control, a lot of your competitors, who have already taken the oars, are going to pull themselves past you.

Guerrilla Marketing With Technology is merely the title of a book. But guerrilla marketing without technology is either not guerrilla marketing at all or it's a major mistake.

Acknowledgments

It took a lot of bright and enthusiastic people to transform this book into the reality you're holding in your hands. Do I mention Vivian Scott first because she is the executive producer of Microsoft's *America at Work* video series from which this book was spawned? I remember how she smiled and her eyes widened at the meeting at which the idea of an online book was proposed. I know I want to thank Bill Gates because his company had the farsightedness to publish this book online at their web site. It may be the very first interactive book in history.

That's why right up front I want to thank every reader of this book who took the time to e-mail me while the chapters were being published online. Their questions helped shape the book, and some of their questions and my answers to them, are published in the upcoming pages.

Certainly my hat should be tipped in gratitude to Linda Mitchell, who invited me to join Microsoft's Small Business Council, thereby turning me on to them and vice versa. Undoubtedly I owe an enormous debt of appreciation to Ray Zambroski at Microsoft; he was my point man and kept things on track for me. And there is no question that Erin Hiraoka helped with her insights about web publishing, not to mention technology and marketing. Erin once said to me, "I am so much in love!" When I asked with whom, she said, "With technology!" Now I can see more clearly where she's coming from.

I thank Brian Labree of Microsoft for knowing the answers to every technical question that ever came up and explaining them to me in ways I could understand. Michele Bourdon came in at the end to keep things shipshape.

Along with my indebtedness to those incredibly nice people at Microsoft, which turned out to be the most gracious company with which I've ever been in contact, I owe a ton of appreciation to my agents, Mike Larsen and Elizabeth Pomada, who said, "You want to publish this book online before it goes to bookstores?", and then proceeded to make that possible.

Robert Michael Pope was the inspiration for the whole idea of monthly chapters, online publishing, and me getting cozy with technology in the first place. A supernova in cyberspace, he is also a galaxy of information. Candace Lynn Jones is no slouch when it comes to information either. She helped brighten the dark times. My daughter, Amy, once asked, "Dad, do you think you'll ever write a book about technology?" My answer was no, but that just goes to show how much smarter kids are than their parents. Speaking of kids, I offer gratitude to three of them—Sage Leila Schofield, Seth Meyer Robert Pickett, and Natalie Sophia Smith—for their toys forced me into technology many a Christmas Eve.

As always, I thank my wife Pat, for allowing me the freedom to have a square-headed mistress with wires and chips. Luckily, Pat has enough self-esteem not to be threatened by my love affair with technology, which is not much of a looker but is loaded with brains and charm.

Finally, bowing with deep gratitude and wishing I could pin a medal on his jacket for having the guts to publish an interactive book that's been seen for free online, I thank Nicholas Philipson, my editor at Addison-Wesley. He transcended the role of editor in this book, acting as a true visionary, then diving into sidebars, appendixes, organization, questions, answers, and design with passion and brilliance.

What a break for me to have been helped so much by so many people!

chapter 1

The Unfair Advantage

Today, success as an entrepreneur is easier to achieve than ever. Americans by the millions have discovered why. They've discovered that almost everything in small business has changed during the past ten years, leaving the little guy with a secret weapon that gives him—and her—an unfair advantage.

Easy-to-use, easy-to-afford technology enables the little guys to appear as large, as expert, and as important as the big guys, to market with the power and dazzle of the titans. Small businesses can now wow their prospects and customers with full-color brochures, visually exciting newsletters, animated web sites—and the list is growing. The technology to produce these marketing weapons was traditionally reserved for the big spenders. But now it is in the domain of the guerrilla marketer. Truth is, it's the guerrilla's secret weapon.

With absolutely zero background in technology, an entrepreneur can now enter arenas once off-limits due to high cost, and win business and profits with effective marketing weapons borne of technology: online focus groups, international marketing partners, data-laden customer lists, and lots more. These weapons are accessible at the click of a mouse or the pressing of a return key.

What the heck is easy-tech?

My name for this technology is "easy-tech," because although it produces results usually associated with the highest of high tech, it may be mastered and used with incredible skill even by low-tech business owners. I ought to know; I am one of the lowest.

I've word-processed with a computer since 1983, sold my books in over 50 nations through the Internet on my own web site, published a newsletter since 1984, hosted a myriad of online conferences and chat sessions, written an online marketing column for three years, coauthored four books while communicating with my coauthors only online, even coauthored three books about cyberspace, but I've still never peered into a computer manual, taken a computer course, or received instruction on what makes my computer work. I don't even care why it works. I only care that it's easy for me to use.

I certainly would have opted for instruction if my immense ignorance had stopped me. But it never did—so I never did. Hey, I don't know why my car works either, but I can drive it.

 ## So much is coming down the pike!

There are many new technologies coming down the pike these days, so many that it's easy to be overwhelmed and decide to resist all of them. Bad idea. For the rest of your life, change will be rapid and prices for technology will drop. It's true that some technology companies have as many as four product cycles in a single year, each of which makes the products of the previous cycle outdated. That can discourage you from making a commitment. But eventually you're going to have to dive into the potent flow of advancement if you're to succeed in your own business. The sooner, the better. Wait too long and the waters will truly be over your head.

This book isn't going to examine all the technologies that are blossoming today, only those that can be of immediate use to small business owners. Guerrillas are rarely as interested in the distant horizon technologies as they are in here and now technologies. They are always fascinated by ways to eliminate errors, increase speed and efficiency, add to their effectiveness, generate new profits for their business, and allow for more balance in their lives—for they know life is more than business.

They do not view technology as an end in itself, though much of the technology is remarkably enticing, and most guerrillas would readily admit that deep down they find using the technology a blast in itself. Instead, they see technology as the means to an end—the end of enjoying their work so much that the journey becomes the goal.

The weapons of technology

Technology allows guerrillas to market and to interact with customers through newsletters, brochures, flyers, web sites, catalogs, faxes, direct mail, research questionnaires, and signs. These are the weapons of technology.

Where geography once limited guerrillas to their own community, the Internet allows them to compete in the global community. Where once they had to deal with the time demands and perils of commuting, and the constraints of a professional wardrobe, their home office has cut their commute down to a stroll and changed their attire from conventional to comfy. They're spending more time with their families. They're spending less time at work.

The technological change that is happening all around us represents not so much a state of revolution as a new permanent condition. It's not going to go away. It's only going to get better. No matter how long you wait, there will still be something more advanced and less costly coming up in an instant. During that instant, though, there are many customers to be attracted and generous profits to be earned. If you don't attract and earn them, somebody else will. And they'll use technology to do it.

There's a person at each end

Guerrillas have learned, to their delight, that technology has far less to do with machines than it does with people. When you're communicating online with someone, you're not connecting with a machine; you're connecting with a person. You're only using a machine to do it. Keep in mind that telephones aren't all about electricity; they're all about people. Few of us can explain how telephones work, but all of us can make a phone call.

Okay, I admit that I was once a serious techno-phobe. Why do you suppose I never cracked the cover of a computer user manual? I thought I'd get a migraine by the second page. And you know something? I was probably right. I didn't need a techno-shrink. I merely needed easier technology. And now I have it. You do too. The doors to profits and free time have been opened for you not by technology per se but by easy-to-use technology. If you've resisted technology, as I did, you'll now find it irresistible, as I did. And a lot of fun, as I do.

Easy-tech lets you replace your fears with self-confidence. It lets you do in 30 minutes what used to take 30 hours. Ever think you, personally, could design a spiffy looking newsletter in as short a time as half an hour? Well, you can. Ever think you could create your own web site from scratch? No? Think again. Easy-tech lets low-tech people utilize high-tech guerrilla marketing weapons.

Is that fair? Darned right it's fair! Small businesses have long been prohibited from taking on the Goliaths due to the high price of admission to the competitive fray. But technology is to small business as the slingshot was to David. It's about time something came along to improve the little guy's odds on the battlefield. And that's just what technology does.

 ## Does high technology mean high anxiety?

As complex as computers used to be when they took up an entire room, that's how simple they are today, when they take up an entire lap. High technology no longer means high anxiety. But technology itself doesn't do the trick. It never does. A guerrilla is needed to breathe life into what technology can do. Guerrillas, such as those you'll read of in this book, are using

DEAR JAY,
I'm not one to argue with a guru like yourself, but computers for me have been all that you proclaim them to be as well as a major drain on my time. Maybe it's wasteful, but I find myself spending untold hours "dinking" around on my Pentium 133. I love it for all the advantages it brings into my life, but I probably spend an inordinate amount of time gazing into its hypnotic monitor. I have found that with all it can do for me, especially with the huge amounts of information now available via CD-ROM and the Internet, I just can't seem to get enough of it and find it difficult to break its spell. — Rick

DEAR RICK,
I hear you talking and I know how much discipline it takes to keep your computer in the proper context. It's a whale of a lot of fun to watch TV, but we manage to limit our time watching. Same goes for driving. It's a real hoot to me, but I usually use my car strictly for transportation. Computers can be used or abused, too, and it does take discipline not to abuse them by spending too much time tinkering with them or surfing endlessly. I suggest you give in to your computer fascination, but only for a specified number of hours each week. Give yourself, say, two or three hours solely for dinking, gazing, playing, and surfing, and then use your computer strictly for business purposes. I admit that I have to use restraint daily to attend to my tasks at hand rather than going off on an extensive cyberjourney, but I seem to have found the right balance after a few months of trying. — Jay

All Q&As have been adapted from electronic dialogue with Jay Levinson at the Microsoft Small Business web site at http://www.microsoft.com/smallbiz.

technology to shape their destinies, redefine and extend their boundaries, achieve and surpass their goals.

America is working in a new way. Small business is not only growing at a faster pace than ever, with more than 2 million start-ups in 1996, it is also succeeding at a higher rate than ever.

Home-based businesses are skyrocketing! Full-time and part-time home-based businesses number 24.3 million. Link Resources reports that 95 percent of these businesses will survive. That's no typo. Only 5 percent of home-based enterprises have bitten the dust each year from 1994 to 1996. The success rate is far higher than that of non-home-based businesses. Every 11 seconds, another home-based biz starts up. Average income of a home-based business owner: $50,250. Average income in the U.S.: $26,000.

 ## The upside to downsizing

The massive downsizing that has destroyed the dreams of so many families has had an upside. It has forced many people into forming businesses of their own, discovering that new technology is simpler and less expensive than they thought, and that it puts success within their grasp.

Lest you think I'm saying technology is your guarantee of success, you're reading me wrong. Running your own business requires self-discipline. It requires a sense of organization. It demands determination. And it's not for everybody. You don't have a boss to keep you on track. You must keep all the promises you make to yourself. If you can live with those parameters, then technology can help ease your way. It can help save you from that dread affliction of the self-employed—workaholism—by saving your time. The key is to keep technology as your tool and not let it become your master.

All the technology I've been referring to will run you less than $4,000. That covers the cost of a good computer to serve as your techno-centerpiece, a speedy modem to transport you throughout cyberspace and also enable you to send and receive faxes, a laser printer so that your documents have credibility, a scanner so that you can add graphic touches to your communications, and a phone line dedicated solely to your business technology. And finally, you'll want the computer software to give wings to your dreams. Want to invest more than $4,000 in your bright future? Okay. But you don't have to. You can also invest a lot of money in your marketing. But you don't have to—if you're a guerrilla.

Just what is guerrilla marketing?

Guerrilla marketing works by having you invest your time, energy, and imagination where you might otherwise invest money. It asks that you base your performance on profits, not sales. It suggests that you establish your goals by the number of relationships you make, not the number of dollars you take in. It urges you to concentrate on following up with existing customers every bit as much as developing new customers.

It encourages you to snuggle up to technology now more than ever, because technology can help you make your way through a business environment that is more competitive than ever. With umpteen million existing businesses and more than 2 million new businesses competing for their attention, customers are more demanding than ever. They want speed and convenience. Technology lets you offer these benefits to them. Or else.

Guerrilla marketing advocates that instead of being bent on competition and wanting to obliterate your competitors, you should be oriented toward cooperation and wanting to co-market with other businesses. Technology makes it easier to spot potential allies, easier to communicate with them, and easier to work with them. Upcoming chapters of this book will investigate how to do this.

What else is in this book?

In chapter 2 you'll get a good look at the virtues of being virtual, the benefit of which is that you no longer need to be limited by geography and can connect to your work resources and customers by technology. In chapter 3 we'll examine the tricks of successfully marketing a small business, with or without technology, although technology does give you new

DEAR JAY,
I would like to submit a question that has stumped me for several months. This problem is also the number one problem I hear in my investigating of this matter with others. How do I determine what I can do as a home business? I have talked with many people about this and they all have the same question. I have read all the articles about doing research in your area to determine what services are needed, market your hobby, buy a franchise, etc. But I have not been able to determine a need in our community that is not already being met. I work full time and do not really have a hobby that is marketable. Franchises are for the most part very expensive and I have limited funds, although I know that loans are available, but that would only load me with more bills that I would not be able to repay if the business did not do well.

I am interested in a home business to supplement my income at the present and my retirement in the future. I do have a good computer and have been learning my way around the Internet, which I enjoy. I have considered some type of computer service such as billing for doctors, or some type of service on the Internet through a web page or bulletin board but do not know how or where to begin. — Sonia

DEAR SONIA,
Your problem is common. The best way to answer your own question is to ask yourself what kind of work you might do if money was not a concern. Then, try to do that work. You will bring to it both interest and enthusiasm, which are cornerstones of all successful businesses.

strengths and capabilities to achieve and surpass your goals.

Marketing is only part of the process in running a business that lives up to your most optimistic expectations.

You mention that some things you might do are already being done by others. But are they being done with the same excellence that you would provide? Would you do anything better than they do? If you think you could improve on the current offerings, you should seriously consider entering that market in spite of the competition. By all means, establish your own web site using easy-tech software, which makes designing your own site both easy and inexpensive. Then, address yourself to finding as many links as possible from related sites to your own, and promote your site in all of your other marketing.

Your idea about helping doctors with billing is a lot like the business of using online communications to serve as the liaison between doctors and insurance companies—a business that has generously rewarded many of those who have entered it.

If you don't know where to begin, let me give you a nudge. Use a search vehicle such as Lycos, Yahoo, Alta Vista, or Magellan to study existing topics that interest you and to locate businesses centered on these topics. Many such businesses may be operating in a geographic area far from yours, allowing you to operate the same enterprise in your own locality. Try to locate newsgroups or bulletin boards that focus on your area of interest, then study them in a quest to find an unmet need. Perhaps you're just the person to fill that need.

The Internet opens up a new world of possibilities and your familiarity with it gives you a head start. The more you surf the Net with an eye toward spotting good opportunities for yourself, the more likely you are to find one. I sure hope you do, and I'm optimistic that you will. — Jay

Another is the care and feeding of customers. The more you understand how to treat them, the better they'll treat you— and that means repeat business, referral business, testimonials and glowing word-of-mouth. So we'll take a detailed look at customers in chapter 4.

Once you're up to speed on marketing and customer care, it's time to dive deep into the waters of technology, to get up close and personal with the benefits technology can offer. In chapter 5, I'll take you by the hand and guide you through that dive so that you're comfortable and at home in such a new environment, proceeding not too fast, not too slow, but at the perfect pace for your company right now and in the future.

DEAR JAY,

Do we continue to wait for investing in technology or do we take our best shot at whatever is available now and hope it doesn't become obsolete in a few months? I run an entrepreneur center in New York. I continue to advise them to use technology for their new business. However, the pursuit of the most advanced technology is not, in my opinion, the answer to their questions. A Pentium 200 could become just an expensive piece of furniture unless the business owner uses every single electronic board in that tool to execute the job. I am using the computer I bought in 1993. I continue to upgrade a bit at a time hoping to take the leap into new super equipment. But you know what? I manage to write articles for the paper, merge three or four mailings a week, e-mail potential customers, and play a CD while drawing in my very same old computer. Either we spend time chasing technology or we learn to use it to run our business effectively. You are the guerrilla guy. Am I on track? — Martha

DEAR MARTHA,

Yes, yes, yes! You are on track and your thinking about technology is in keeping with the guerrilla mindset.

Next, we'll look into one of your most precious resources, which happens to be one of the most misunderstood of all the riches bestowed upon humankind. I'm talking about time. And chapter 6 talks about how to save and make the most of it. That chapter will also get you to stop believing a lie you've probably believed all your life: that time is money.

Chapter 7 will attempt to change your focus from competing to collaborating, from hoarding to sharing. It will open your mind to the vast number of allies who can help you if only you'll plug into the technology that can bring them aboard.

Waiting to invest in improving technology is an endless wait because technology will continue to improve, become more powerful, and cost less as time goes by. By using technology to its fullest potential, you will be able to capture markets that would be taken by others if you chose to wait.

This doesn't mean you must always stay on the "bleeding edge" of hardware advancement; if you invest in enough hardware up front, you can keep up with software upgrades and improvements over several years, and that's the key to staying productive and getting the most from your technology investment. Entrepreneurs are much better off doing what you suggest: learning to maximize the benefits of current technology, upgrading when they can't do what's necessary to be effective or competitive, and maintaining their marketing activities with the same zeal that you are.

The idea is not to chase technology but to use what exists to its utmost. Businesses rarely rise or fall because of the machines they own. They succeed because of the owners' attitude, passion, and ability to get the most from those machines. — Jay

Have I mentioned the Internet yet? Amazing that I haven't, because it's a glorious marketing opportunity, getting better daily, and it can propel you to your dreams. Some people think it's like a tidal wave and we're all sitting around in kayaks. Chapter 8, about the Net, will get you from that kayak and into a seaworthy frame of mind that will make navigating and harvesting the Internet as profitable as it is pleasurable.

With you feeling at home in cyberspace, it will be time to scrutinize those magical places where technology has an impact on marketing. Chapter 9 first identifies ten such places, then reveals 27 specific weapons that technology can put into your marketing arsenal.

What is on the horizon for the small business owner armed with the powers of technology and the wisdom of the guerrilla? Chapter 10 peers at that horizon, then over it to get a good perspective on where small business will fit in the future. You'll love that future if you're ready for it.

 ## The rules are changing and that's not all

Small business is changing because the rules are changing. The sophistication of the consumer is changing. The way people buy is changing. Communications are changing. Expectations are changing. And the emphasis put on time is changing. Time is more important now than ever, and will only continue to increase in importance. The prime purpose of technology is to save precious time.

Many of the advantages granted by easy-tech were never before available to small business. Saving time, reaching new markets, marketing globally, competing with giants, customizing marketing, dazzling customers with service and caring, and making quantum leaps in efficiency weren't really options for the one-man bands of yesteryear. But the easy-tech of today puts these options within the reach of most small businesses. Some will ignore new technology and hope it disappears. Others will use it before their competitors to thrive and flourish in a changed world.

America at work used to conjure up the sounds of laborers grunting, wagon wheels rolling, machines clanging, and factory whistles blaring. Now America at work is the sound of people gabbing at their local coffeehouse, the sound of computer keyboards clacking, the sound of modems clicking, and the sound of music playing in the background of the home office.

chapter 2

The Virtual Guerrilla

All my dictionaries seem to agree that the definition of virtual is "existing in essence or effect though not in actual fact." Funny that I had to look it up, because I've been a virtual guerrilla for over a quarter century. That means I've been working from an office, but that office has sometimes been taking a 20-day drive from Chicago to San Francisco, or overlooking the ski slopes high in the wintry mountains of Montana, or on a delightful cruise to Rio.

Virtual these days means *connected through technology.* Guerrillas, wherever they toil, stay connected to their customers, their bosses, their employees, their suppliers, and other guerrillas. They're also more connected to their families, their friends, their communities, and to the best that is in themselves. Guerrillas realize that we're not really moving toward the twenty-first century; it's moving toward us. And we've got to be ready for it or it will sweep over us, leaving us in its wake.

Virtual is a state of mind

As that twenty-first century looms on the near horizon, we see that virtual refers to a work style, a lifestyle, a state of mind. It puts people more in control of their lives than they are in a nonvirtual setting. It offers a glorious sense of freedom, remarkable flexibility for employees and customers, and perhaps most winning of all, it might permit you to commute in your slippers. In most cases, that means a stroll from your bedroom to your home office—unless you've set up your office in your bedroom. In that case, you've got the shortest of all possible commutes.

Of course, being virtual doesn't always mean being at home. Many virtual businesses are run from real offices in real office buildings. Actually, they're run from anywhere small business owners please. Some are constantly on the move. Many innovative, creative, independent spirits cherish the freedom of not having to be chained to one place. They appreciate the flexibility of being connected from wherever is convenient for them or their customers. Whether their connections are wired or wireless, their mindset is that of the guerrilla: work doesn't care where it's accomplished if it's accomplished with excellence. Virtual offices help small business and big business, home-based or office-based, stationary or mobile.

The first virtual office may have been the one set up in 1877 by a bank president who put up a phone line between his office in Boston and his home in nearby Somerville. He used technology. He was connected. He had the right idea.

Today a burgeoning 23 percent of the working population in the United States have that same idea. They are mobile workers, users of technology, connected. In the nineties alone, over 12 million people have decided to work from home. The total number now enjoying the benefits of working where they live is up to 39 million, according to IDC/Link, a marketing research firm. In my part of the planet in Northern California, one out of six people has a home-based business.

That seems to prove that the virtual office isn't in the far future, a figment of science fiction. It's here with us right this very moment, all over the place. Many big organizations are now encouraging employees to set up virtual offices. The Internet provides global opportunities and the chance to render 24-hour service. It also helps satisfy employees' desire for the freedom of virtuality. Experts say that an employee who works at home two days a week saves a company $12,000 a year.

Because of the economic and humanitarian benefits, the number of home-based virtual offices in the U.S. is expected to grow by 20 percent each year through the year 2000. Virtual offices based outside the home will account for another huge amount of growth. Technology is improving by getting easier and more affordable. Batteries are getting smaller and more powerful. The Internet is flourishing, yet still in its infancy. The wireless age is dawning, proving that you don't need wires to be wired.

 ## A little help from your friends

Those who confine their commuting to a virtual office, home-based or otherwise, are known as telecommuters. They have opted for a life, not of independence, which you may associate with a virtual office, but of interdependence, knowing that they get by with a little help from their friends—a lot of friends, in the guise of independent contractors, who are really interdependent contractors helping each other.

Some have their virtual offices at home, while others have them in an office building, and still others in their car, their van, their RV, their boat. Even their Harley? Yep, even there. If you're connected, you're connected. Some work alone while others share offices. And all are connected.

Increasing numbers of small businesses, from travel agents to doctors, from manufacturers to bookstores, are realizing the joys of virtuality even though they don't necessarily think of themselves as virtual. But they're so networked with the world and their allies that they only look traditional from the outside. Instead they are the essence of technology. The keys to their success reside in their connections, in being virtual.

My virtual office connects me to pretty much the same people and places I was connected to when I was in a nonvirtual office. Only it connects me from a better place than ever before, my home. And I get to take my office with me, for the most part, when I leave home—if I want.

At first my virtual office consisted of a phone, desk, and typewriter. If you looked at it you'd easily have mistaken it for a dining room. Now, in a different city, a different state, and a different setting, it still looks a lot more like our family dining room—and sometime poker parlor—than it does an office. It's traditional in its look, but virtual in its heart.

 ## What's in a virtual office?

These days my virtual office consists of a phone, desk, fax modem, computer, printer, copier, cell phone, car phone, and subscriptions to a couple of online services so I can benefit from the delightful speed and convenience of e-mail—and access the information superlibrary known as the Internet. An important part of my office is my charge account with Federal Express.

When I'm even more virtual, my office may boast a laptop computer, a pager, possibly even a digital notepad or a wireless PDA (personal digital assistant). I might opt for a scanner so I can incorporate graphics into my work. For now, my office does a dandy job of connecting me to information, people, and services almost anywhere in the world and at any time I want.

The key point here is "any time I want." When I'm in my car, I never get calls on my car phone because nobody knows my number. I don't want to take calls while I'm driving. If I want to be reached, I can simply give my number. But I never have. If I want to be cut off from the universe, I can be. The joy of a virtual office is that it can be up and running whenever you want, and it can be disconnected from the world whenever you want. As a virtual guerrilla, you've got the option.

When I started working from my virtual office, the first thing I had to do was to explain to my wife and daughter that, even though I was at home, I was working. I may have been clad in Levi's and a T-shirt, but I was accomplishing tasks that would bring in the money to pay the bills. If we all hadn't become perfectly clear about that, my working from home would have gone awry. But my wife learned to ignore me, and my daughter and her friends learned to keep down the racket, during my working hours.

Even though I can work from wherever I want, I must admit that home is my favorite place. I know I can pop my cellular phone in my attaché case and work from the beach, but I find it hard to work from there. Ditto for working from the places where I take holidays. Still, it's nice to know I can if I want.

 ## The benefits of a virtual office

I study the benefits of running a virtual office and I see that every one of them is true for my life. Increased revenue? It's more than twice what it was before I was virtual. Increased productivity? I can now accomplish in three days what used to take five. In fact, I've been working a three-day week from my virtual office since 1971. Better customer service? Ask my clients and publishers. Increased revenue opportunities? No question about it, especially since I've begun surfing in cyberspace. Improved morale? Ask my wife and daughter. Ask me. The answer is yes.

Virtual workers enjoy these benefits whether they work at home or in an office. Dell Computer and Amazon.com are two examples of wildly successful companies that are incredibly virtual yet not home-based—very high-tech acting on the inside but pretty down-to-earth looking on the outside. Dell is one of the largest computer makers on earth and Amazon is the single largest bookseller on that same earth. Both are virtual—that is, connected. Both are relatively new. Both are typical of many other businesses that are free of geographic restraints. Think of an elephant with the speed and agility of a cheetah. That's what being virtual means to them.

The downside of going virtual

You often hear that the downside of a home office is loneliness. One of my favorite facts of the nineties is that the rapid growth in home offices is paralleled in only one other industry: coffeehouses. It seems that people who work in virtual settings do long for face-to-face contact, and they get it at their

DEAR JAY,
My question is one that many consultants have asked me and has to do with proposing the virtual office concept to a client. For example, when I receive a call from an agency or a client, I sometimes propose "working off-site." A few clients are fine with this and we have done great work for them. My question is: Can you provide some key points to make in dealing with clients or agencies to encourage them to be more comfortable/accepting of this concept? Although we are slowly building some clients that have experienced our work off-site (away from the client and working at home), many consultants and developers I talk to haven't. In trying to persuade clients to accept a virtual arrangement, we usually refer to our office setup mentioning equipment, communications gear, books, etc., and the costs of that setup the client won't have to provide. Sometimes I mention that I can meet with them once a week if needed, to discuss work performed and get feedback. What is a list of dos and don'ts in conversing with a client in order to present the concept/idea of performing work for them off-site? Many of us would appreciate some detailed ideas you may have on this. — Jeff

DEAR JEFF,
In order for your clients to understand the wisdom and benefits of being virtual and allowing you to work

neighborhood coffeehouse. As for me, I get all the socializing I need during the days when I'm not in my virtual office.

The virtual office does not have a glass ceiling. It offers a higher quality of life by giving workers more control over their time and their work environment; by reducing the time spent commuting and the stress associated with commuting; by linking workers with a broad spectrum of professional colleagues,

off-site, you should stress three things: (1) Being virtual can increase a client's profitability by decreasing operating expenses—commuting costs, office space, and more—by having employees/contracted employees working at home. That's what to emphasize, because profitability is the name of the game and what is probably on all clients' minds. If you relate virtuality to their profitability, you'll find it easier to make your point. (2) Being virtual can save the client's time— nobody is ever caught in that horrible traffic jam on the freeway, correspondence is microseconds away— and extra time results in extra productivity. Most clients will like the idea of gaining this extra time because they'll equate it with their profits. If they don't, you should point this out to them. (3) Being virtual is growing across America in businesses of all types because it makes so much sense. Easy-to-use technology is why this is happening, and once businesses see the benefits of using it, they hardly ever return to their pre-virtual ways.

You might also let your clients know that once they become more virtual, it will be easier for them to attract better employees by offering them the flexibility granted by working from a virtual office. In addition, they'll most likely be able to reduce their overhead. I think it's a great idea for you to meet with them once a week as they wean themselves from one century to the next. — Jay

thereby making work more interesting; and by helping work to go more efficiently so that workers have more time for the things that help them achieve balance in their lives. The virtual office does not require a high overhead. But it does require an enormous discipline. Without a boss or an associate to remind you of an impending deadline, you've got to remind yourself, then meet it.

I do three things to keep myself disciplined:

1. I write tasks on my daily calendar, knowing they are promises I make to myself and that I don't ever want to lie to myself.

2. I remind myself of the carrot at the end of the stick: a four-day weekend. I am powerfully motivated to keep my promises to myself because I know that if I don't, my weekend is shorter.

3. I cross tasks off my calendar. I get immense joy from this, and a sense of bliss when they're all crossed off. I've learned that behaving virtually isn't an event, but a habit. Meeting and beating deadlines is a way of life for me.

After all, a goal is only a dream with a deadline. And working from your own home, calling your own shots, certainly is a dream existence for many. The promise of being able to work from home is one of the ways that many guerrilla enterprises are attracting superb employees.

 ## If you're tempted, be careful

If you're tempted to go virtual yourself, be sure you don't run afoul of any zoning laws, landlords, or neighbors. Make certain that you've got enough electrical power to support your computer, fax modem, copier and other virtual gadgets. You never want to make a photocopy that ends up turning off the power in your whole neighborhood. Don't laugh. It has happened.

Virtually Growing a Business

A father and son flower wholesaling business in Las Vegas does all its work on the road. Supplying over a third of the city's 140 florists, they started out in a small cargo van, delivering fresh flowers from a group of growers on California's central coast. As their reputation as dependable suppliers of high-quality flowers grew, they realized that a minimal investment in technology (not to mention a larger truck) would enable them to compete more effectively by offering value-added products to customers and making more efficient use of their time.

A laptop computer with plug-in capabilities, and a beeper, have turned their truck (which also serves as a mobile showroom) into a virtual office. The beeper allows customers to place special requests at any time. The laptop can be taken right into each flower shop, allowing the wholesalers to access customers' accounts, check on flower availability and prices, take orders, and print accurate invoices on the spot.

Meanwhile, armed with databases and an accounting program, the laptop becomes an indispensable tool during the six-hour drive to California or between customer calls, as the wholesalers update customer accounts, run financial reports, and catch up on correspondence and other administrative duties. The net result of this highly flexible and efficient operation is an increase in business volume and profits.

To have a virtual office, you've got to have the proper space for it. You need a practical desk and a comfortable chair, along with decent lighting. You've also got to have at least a modicum of privacy. Other than that, it seems to come down to the three "w's": water, wits, and being wired. To those, you might also add the three "d's": discipline, determination, and details. You've got to keep those promises you make to yourself. You've got to realize that success means being knocked down 15 times and getting back to your feet 15 times. And you must have a sense of organization that prohibits you from overlooking anything. As the wise person said, "God is in the

All case example sidebars have been adapted from the six-part *America at Work* video series, produced by Microsoft Corporation's Small Business Group, 1996.

details." Speaking of details, the current tax laws say your home office can be deductible if your major income comes from self-employment or if you can prove your employer requires that you work from home.

 ## The measurements of a virtual office

The better you are at being virtual, the more streamlined you are. That translates into saving time and generating profits. In fact, the measurements of your venture into virtuality are your effectiveness, profits, speed, and morale. That includes the morale of your customers.

Every guerrilla should be part of a network of guerrillas. And your network should include some people who are virtual already. Their familiarity with the terrain can help you. You probably won't find all you need in your community, but you'll probably find a lot more than you need scattered around the world. I've teamed up on major projects, working from my virtual office and using my modem, fax, and phone, with guerrillas in San Francisco, Sedona, Denver, New York, Boston, and Jakarta. I met those teammates face-to-face no more than once during the sometimes year-long projects. We only met when we did because we wanted to, not because we had to.

 ## The more technology, the more you're connected

As you're beginning to glean, being virtual means using technology. The more technology, the more connected you are. A Coopers & Lybrand survey of fast-growing small businesses revealed that revenue per employee is two and a half times higher for companies that are using today's technology than for those ignoring it.

That technology helps keep you organized, puts all of your work in one place no matter where you happen to be, and contributes mightily to your overall efficiency. The results are more productivity, better service, and increased profitability for your business. Technology also makes you more desirable as a partner to your fellow guerrillas and as a supplier to your customers.

But technology isn't the only secret weapon of guerrillas who dwell in virtual offices. You can have all the latest technology in the world and still fall on your virtual keister if you aren't armed with the proper attitudes for succeeding in a virtual way. Not surprisingly, the attitudes necessary for victory on this battlefield are the same as those necessary for success at guerrilla marketing.

Arming yourself with the attitudes

These ten attitudes are every bit as important to your virtual existence as the speed and efficiency you'll enjoy from the machines you add to your arsenal:

1 **You operate according to a plan** Your plan is brief, clear, and able to guide your business as well as your marketing. You create this plan with your goals in mind, base most of your decisions upon it, and review it regularly. Everyone who works with you should read and understand the plan. Ideally, they even helped you formulate it at the outset. Your plan even lists the ways you will become more and more virtual with time.

2 **You grow your business by a calendar** It's a calendar that you have created, outlining your marketing plans for the next year, week by week. This makes decision making a simpler process. It helps you see into the future. It encourages you to be proactive rather than reactive. At the end of the year, you see how the marketing activities on your calendar affected your profits, and you make a better calendar for the next year.

3 **You are the essence of flexibility** You know that customer service is anything the customer wants it to be.

Nobody has to tell you that quality is the price of admission to small business success and that flexibility is a competitive advantage upon which you may hang your hat. In an era of increasingly sophisticated customers, if you can't bend, you'll break. You've learned that the more technology you embrace, the more flexibility you can offer.

4 **you are a giver and not a taker** You are known to give valuable things away. You offer free consultations, demonstrations, samples. You may give seminars or clinics. You provide free information, brochures, newsletters. You give gifts to customers and often to prospects who request more data. You may write a column or an article for a local paper or an Internet service—at no charge. You give speeches about your industry to local groups. No wonder people are attracted to your business. You know that we're smack dab in the middle of the Information Age, and you've learned that the Internet is brimming with information your customers would love. You mine the Internet for data and freely share it.

5 **your business has credibility** Everything connected to your business looks professional and inspires confidence in you. Your stationery, business cards, brochures, flyers, even your business forms, show that you've got substance and style, that you can be trusted. Your phone is answered in a way that makes callers feel good. Your office may be virtual, but your excellence is real.

6 **you embrace the spirit of competitiveness** You realize deep in your bones that no matter what business others may think you're in, you're really in the marketing business. That means you tingle at the very idea of launching a guerrilla marketing attack with a myriad of weapons, many of which you can create right there in your virtual office.

7 **you are alert for fusion opportunities** As a guerrilla, you are as alert to cooperation as you are to competition. You keep your entrepreneurial radar attuned to fusion opportunities in marketing, services, data, technology, even office space. As you network your virtual office with others in the world of interdependent guerrillas, the concept of "I'll scratch your back if you scratch mine" keeps you itch free.

8 **You are at ease with technology** You know that it's all simpler to use than ever, that it is no longer a luxury but is now an absolute necessity. The newest of the new does not intimidate you because you're learning that technology is adapting to users by becoming so friendly, it's almost cordial. Whoever thought you'd be a desktop publisher, a database manager, an online information analyst? I did. And you are.

9 **You are the very soul of follow-up** "Relationships" is your middle name. You prove it by the way you're in consistent touch with your customers and prospects by e-mail, snail mail, faxes, and phone calls. You stay in contact with them through newsletters, flyers, postcards, and letters. They know you're also easy to contact, and their loyalty to you is as real as you are virtual.

10 **You feel passion about your work** That passion fuels your desire to learn about your customers, please them, surpass their expectations. It is a passion that extends to those who work with you, to your suppliers, to your fusion partners. It is readily apparent in the way you run your virtual office, embracing the speed and economy it offers you as a business as well as the freedom and achievement it offers you as a person.

Although it's certainly not for everybody, the virtual office is rapidly becoming the office of today. Your most precious resources are your time, your freedom, and your potential. A virtual office, whether in a suburban home or a downtown office building, can contribute to your ability to save, use, and invest your time wisely; to gain more precious freedom to do anything you want; and to get closer in touch with your true potential.

chapter 3

Marketing Your Small Business

Regardless of the business you're in, you're really in the marketing business. If you produce a first-rate product or render a blue-ribbon service, your quality will exist in a vacuum if you don't market your offerings with the skill and aplomb of a guerrilla.

Guerrillas seek conventional goals using unconventional methods. They invest their own time, energy, and imagination into the marketing process if they don't have a lot of money, which they usually don't. They understand how marketing works, and that it's a process rather than an event. They know that time is the ally of the guerrilla and not the enemy. A well-crafted marketing plan improves over time, but most small business owners lack the patience to invest that time.

What marketing really is

Smart marketers recognize what marketing really is: every single contact that any member or part of your company makes with anyone else. Marketing includes how your phone is answered, the stationery you use, your willingness to follow up, your hours and days of business, the neatness of your premises, and a myriad of details that most people just don't consider to be marketing. Once you recognize these things as marketing, you'll have a head start over the people who don't.

 ## The big boon to small business

Technology is easily the biggest boon to small business marketing in history. It adds firepower to your use of traditional marketing weapons such as newsletters, brochures, flyers, business cards, proposals, signs, gift certificates, flipcharts, and catalogs, because it allows you to produce them professionally yet easily. That gives you the credibility that all small and new businesses need.

It also admits you to the fertile arena of the Internet, a marketing world in itself, and allows you to maintain a customer list that teems with data about each person on it. Current easy-tech enables you to locate and connect with marketing partners throughout the world. It lets you use your computer, telephone, or fax machine as a marketing tool even when you're not around. Technology makes it possible for you to provide the speed and responsiveness that customers of today demand. It also helps you to build better relationships with customers.

For instance, a web page is a great opportunity for you to build a prospective client database. Adding an e-mail response to a web page will allow you to capture the e-mail address of people who are interested in your product or service. In turn, e-mail is a very inexpensive way to send marketing materials to the people who have already expressed interest in your company.

Naturally you've got to know marketing before you market online. You've got to be prepared to respond rapidly to e-mail from customers, to keep your web site fresh and appealing, and to learn how best to interact on the Internet. It's all new terrain, and the sooner you learn how to navigate it, the better. But whatever you do, don't ignore it.

Just one century ago few small businesses realized the impact of the telephone. They couldn't imagine how it could help them achieve profits. Today most businesses would be lost in space if they weren't connected to others by telephone. The same is true of computers and the Internet. Shortsighted business owners, unable to comprehend how technology can help them, adopt a wait-and-see attitude. But while they're waiting, their competitors are seeing the benefits gained through the use of computers and the growing enormity of the online marketplace. Those competitors are snapping up customers and niches, profits and name awareness, while the laggards fade further and further into the distance.

But all the advanced technology on the planet can't produce profits unless that technology is backed by a solid working knowledge of marketing and what makes marketing successful. Technology opens the door to a vast array of weaponry, but unless you know how to aim and fire those weapons, they could end up backfiring.

 ## The principles of guerrilla marketing

Before delving into the weapons of marketing available to guerrillas, it's a good idea to understand the 12 principles that all guerrillas know about marketing with technology—or without technology. If you understand 11 of the principles, you're going to be up against the wall when you compete against businesses that understand and run their businesses by all 12. The idea is to commit all 12 principles to memory, then to run your business as though these concepts are part of your DNA. Here's a memory crutch for you: all 12 principles are based on words ending in the letters "ent."

1 **Commitment makes it happen** The one-word answer to "What makes marketing work?" is *commitment.* Marketing becomes stronger over time because people make most purchase decisions unconsciously. The way to access their unconscious minds is by repetition. It's hard to practice repetition if you don't commit to your marketing plan, if you abandon ship before it has a chance to set sail.

Many brilliant marketing plans have been discarded merely because they didn't generate instant results. But marketing rarely does produce the results you want in a short time. People aren't paying that much attention to marketing, so it takes quite a while for yours to have much of an impact. Just realize that Maytag, one of the best marketed brands of appliances, didn't enjoy sales gains the first year after it switched to using a lonely repairman as its symbol. But today Maytag is a top seller. The reason: commitment to a marketing plan.

I do not love telling you this about marketing, but the truth is this: Mediocre marketing with commitment works a whole lot better than brilliant marketing without commitment. Don't say you haven't been alerted. And don't embark upon a marketing program unless you're prepared to commit to it.

2 **The best investment in America** Putting out money for marketing isn't an expense as much as it is an *investment*. When you market properly—and these 12 principles will tell you how to do that—you'll find that it's the best investment available in America today. It rewards your investment more richly than a lending institution and carries with it less risk than a brokerage house. Once you view any money put into marketing as an investment, you'll be less tempted to walk away from your marketing plan after only a short while.

You'd never buy shares of stock in a company then dump them if the stock dropped a few points. But many small business owners invest in marketing then dump their plans because the marketing doesn't generate results fast enough. Wise investments don't always pay off in a hurry, and marketing, one of the wisest you can make, pays off slowly but surely. That happens only if you stick with your plan. Guerrilla marketing is all about investing in your future, and not about instant results.

3 **The importance of being consistent** The best marketing is always *consistent*. You can vary your headlines, your visuals, and even your offers. But your identity should remain constant. Your niche should remain constant. Your visual format should remain constant. Your theme, your logo, and your media should remain constant. Studies show that it takes nine penetrations of the mind to move a person from total apathy about your business to purchase readiness. For every three times you put out the word, people will be paying attention only one of those times. That means establishing yourself in the minds of your prospects will probably take 27 exposures.

If you change your marketing thrust, the people who are just getting to know you will not know exactly who you are or what you stand for. You may be bored with your marketing, but always remember that your prospects are just getting to know you. The more consistent you are, the more they'll know they can rely upon you. Restraint will be your best friend. Some of the most effective marketing in history has remained relatively unchanged for decades. I call your attention to the good hands of Allstate, the Budweiser Clydesdale horses, the Pillsbury Doughboy, the be-all-that-you-can-be U.S. Army, and the valley of the Jolly Green You-know-who.

4 **Making people confident in you** People patronize businesses in which they are *confident.* Research cited in *Advertising Age* has proved that price is the fifth most important factor for people choosing a business to patronize. Selection is fourth. Service is third. Quality, which you might think would rank number one, really ranks number two. The overwhelming winner in this research is confidence.

Your commitment to your program will make them confident. Treating your marketing as a long-term investment and not walking away from it prematurely will make them confident. Your consistency will make them confident. And if they're confident, they'll most likely become customers. Everything you do with your marketing should be designed to increase confidence in your business.

5 **The patient guerrilla** The most successful marketing is accomplished by people who are *patient.* Of all the personality traits present in people who direct profitable marketing programs, patience is the one most essential to enabling all the others. Only patient people can: practice commitment; view their marketing costs as investments; hang in there and be consistent enough to win the battle for the customer's mind; market to a point that they have earned the confidence of their prospects.

If you're not the patient sort, turn your marketing over to someone who is. The marketing battlefields are littered with winning marketing plans left behind by impatient marketing directors. Even if you have everything else going right for you, your impatience can undermine your goals. Guerrillas are rarely in a hurry.

DEAR JAY,

I just opened a computer learning center six months ago. We had people call requesting class and schedule information. We mailed them the information but didn't do any follow-up. Is it too late to follow up with these customers? Previous customers who have taken a class with us also didn't receive any follow-up. Is it too late for them? By follow-up, I mean a personal phone call. We mail everyone on our customer base a newsletter. But we don't do personal follow-up with the phone. We use newsletters to keep our customers informed, not only about us, but also about computers in general. How long should a good newsletter be? How much should you promote yourself in the newsletter? Too much and it will look like a four- to six-page advertisement. You mentioned using various new technologies—fax, e-mail, web site, newsletter, etc.—and that we should try to use as many as we possibly can to meet the needs of the many. If we limit ourselves to only getting a fax machine, what about the customers who don't have a fax but have e-mail? We might be limiting ourselves if we only use a limited number of weapons. The more weapons we use, the more customers we will accommodate. — Pete

6 **A winning assortment** The days of single-weapon marketing may be behind us. Many small businesses have learned, to their dismay, that advertising just doesn't work. Direct mail doesn't do the trick either. Nor do public relations and telemarketing. Not even marketing on the Internet is sufficient by itself. So what does do the trick? A wide *assortment* of weapons.

When you combine advertising with direct mail, then add public relations and telemarketing, and also market on the Internet, all the weapons work better. It's the combination of weapons that works. People see the ad for your enterprise, then they get your letter. Shortly after this they read a story about your firm in their newspaper. Next they receive a phone

---

DEAR PETE,

About those customers who requested information, follow up on those people as soon as possible. The best time to have followed up was within one week of them contacting you. The less time that elapses, the better. Still, follow-up now is a lot better than none at all. The same is true for those who already took a class with you. If you didn't follow up within a week, do it now. I agree that phone calls are an excellent follow-up method and I suggest staying with that program. When guerrillas market with newsletters, they devote 75 percent of the newsletter, which should be from four to eight pages long, to giving information of worth and value, and 25 percent to selling their products or services. This way, people will look forward to your newsletter instead of considering it one long ad. I'm with you on your perception of technology, too. You should try to match your technology to that of your customers. They aren't all online yet, and most likely some don't even have a fax machine. So you've got to employ e-mail, faxes, phones, and snail mail. The more customers you accommodate, the healthier your business will be. — Jay

call. They've heard about you by this time. They've read about you. When they hear your voice, it is no longer the voice of a complete stranger. If you've got a web site, they can check you out even more. The familiarity that results from this multi-weapon approach makes it much more likely that a customer will eventually buy what you are selling. Did your ad do the job? No way. The assortment of weapons gets the credit. And you get it, too, because you knew that a wide assortment is a winning assortment.

7 **Being profitable by being convenient** A key to profitable marketing is making your company extremely easy to buy from, and knocking yourself out to be a *convenient* business to work with. That means you've got a phone that will be answered twenty-four hours a day, seven days a week. You don't have to be there; your telephone technology can be there for you. It means you offer extended hours of business and happily allow business transactions any day of the week. It means you've got a web site so people can really get to know the details about your business and can ask you questions, knowing they'll get a rapid response. It means you take all credit cards, offer a variety of financing plans, and have abundant free information to send to those who request it.

You also offer convenience with your fax machine and your e-mail address. You don't buy into that myth that time is money. You know it is far more important than money and that if you waste anybody's precious time, they'll find somebody else who respects it.

8 **Marketing subsequent to the sale** Guerrillas are well aware that marketing doesn't end with the sale. They know that's when marketing really begins. The truly big profits come to your company *subsequent* to the sale. All the hard work and effort you put into transforming a prospect into a customer doesn't always get paid off with the first sale. The serious profits come with repeat purchases, referrals, and loyalty that lasts for decades.

It costs six times more to sell something to a new prospect than to an existing customer. As a result, guerrillas mine their customer lists for gold, and they find it with consistent follow-up, never ignoring a customer after a purchase. They know that nearly 70 percent of business lost in America is lost due to apathy after the sale has been consummated. Their assiduous follow-up replaces apathy with loyalty. Their marketing subsequent to the sale breeds a stable of loyal customers. Guerrillas market like crazy to these good people nestled in their database, enthralled at how doing so increases their profits while decreasing their marketing budget.

9 **The amazement of you** There are many fascinating, even amazing things about your business that you may take for granted because you encounter them on a day-to-day basis. But if your prospects and customers knew of these details, they would be impressed. That's why guerrillas always seek to add an element of *amazement* to their marketing. This element makes your company and your offerings interesting. And guerrillas know in their hearts that people don't pay much attention to marketing for its own sake, but they pay rapt attention to things that interest them, and even more attention to things that amaze them.

You traveled to Europe and Asia to obtain goods for sale? Amazing! You've got two people whose only job for you is quality control? Amazing! You spent three years developing and testing your software? Amazing! More than 1,500 people in your community have purchased from you during the past three months? Amazing! There are many details about your business that are astonishing and remarkable. Many of them deliver highly desired benefits to your prospects and customers. Tell the world about the details and the benefits. Amaze the world!

10 **Treasuring measurement** Pay close attention here, because this is where you can actually double your profits. This may be the least glamorous part of marketing, but it ranks high on the scale of importance. I'm talking about *measurement*.

You utilize a variety of marketing weapons, just as a good guerrilla should. Some of those weapons are going to hit the target right in the bullseye. Good for you! Some of them are going to miss the target completely. Bad for you! But are you going to know which is which? Will you know which weapons

DEAR JAY,
Regarding the section on "the amazement of you"— yes, if your product succeeds, people will be amazed. You have to constantly develop your marketing, and only your clients will ultimately inform you how successful your product is or will be. I have a basic query for any business: How do companies go from producing one product to operating as a huge conglomerate, in so little time, and continue to be organized with well-defined goals and the ability to easily adapt to the quick change of market requirements and technologies? — Deepak

DEAR DEEPAK,
When I refer to the amazement of you, I'm talking about communicating in your marketing the amazing things your company does to serve its customers in the best possible way. Big, successful companies grow by being aware of the change that is always around us and by maintaining their focus. They flourish because they are committed to quality and service. It all happens because of a management that is sensitive to market requirements and customer needs. And never underestimate offering the right product at the right time to the right people in the right way. These things aren't easy, but if management feels passionate about the business, their energies fuel the fires of growth and profitability. — Jay

to continue firing and which should be relegated to the annals of history? You will if you track the results of your marketing.

You've got to ask people where they heard of you and determine which of your marketing vehicles got through to them. Many people will say, "A friend told me about you," not mentioning the six ads they've seen, the two letters you mailed, or your web site, at which they spent two hours the other day. People never like admitting they were affected by marketing, so they'll usually credit their purchase to word-of-mouth.

You've got to dig deep and try to pin these people down. If they say they're buying because of a buddy's recommendation, ask if they've seen your ads in the *Daily Gazette* or in the local magazine, *Cityscape,* or heard them on radio stations KFOG or KMEL. Maybe they found you online. Find out just where they learned of you. If you don't, you may end up wasting half your marketing budget, and you won't ever know which half.

11 **The joy of involvement** There's a name for your relationship with your customers. It's *involvement.* You prove you're involved with them by your follow-up. They become more involved with you each time they read your newsletter, receive a note from you, get a phone call, access your web site, or hear of you in the media. They actually sense your involvement with them when they speak to you in person—at their place of business, at trade shows, in the community—or on the phone. You prove that you know about them and care about them.

Customers prove they're involved with you by the way they make repeat purchases, and by the way they readily give you names of people to contact and to add to your mailing list. And let's never forget their delightful inclination to recommend your business to their friends and associates. Your involvement with them makes them even more confident. Their involvement with you makes you even more profitable.

Think of it like this: Not being involved is like hollering across the street to somebody; being involved is like whispering in that person's ear.

12 **Seeking to be dependent** Blending with your thoughts of competition should be thoughts of co-operation, as you develop a radar for businesses that have two characteristics: you can help them and they can help you. With everyone around the world becoming more and more connected to each other, and small business start-ups blossoming like wildflowers, the key concept to embrace is to be *dependent.*

Although many one-person and home-based businesses are flourishing, they're not going it as alone as you may think. Many have linked up with other businesses to provide more services to their customers. Many more barter goods and services for mutual benefit. Even more add firepower to each other's marketing with fusion marketing programs and links on the Internet. Guerrillas have a knack for locating and recruiting brother and sister guerrillas in the quest for profits, some from the list of new start-ups in the community, others from the Fortune 500.

Don't link with enterprises whose standards of product and service are lower than yours, with companies that seem fascinated with the quick buck, with firms that aren't as customer oriented as you are. When you find a likely ally, start by providing links to each other for a short-term experiment, say, two months. If your partner is up to snuff during this period, link for longer. If not, say good-bye.

 ## Easier to point and click to than to do

It's relatively easy for you to recognize these twelve ENT words, nodding affirmatively to each concept in your mind. It's not so simple to live by them.

Commitment is a bear! Imagine sticking with something that doesn't seem to be working out all that well. When do you finally throw up your hands? It's not as soon as most instant-gratification types would like. Thinking of your marketing as an investment isn't a cinch when the returns on it aren't coming in as soon as you hoped they would. Being consistent is a drag when your friends, coworkers, and family, who see your marketing daily, insist that they're bored and you should change everything around. You've got to remember that your prospects barely know you.

Earning enough trust to make people confident in you is, like marketing itself, a process and not an event. Processes take time. It's not easy to be patient for a long time, so if you're not, turn the marketing reins over to someone who is. That person should recognize the limitations of individual marketing weapons and know that the weapons need each other to achieve their maximum effectiveness. Guerrilla marketing is about seriously considering all the weapons, testing many of them, then ending up with a proven assortment of them. Not easy. Looking at your business through the eyes of a customer to determine how convenient it is to do business with you is simple enough, but wait till you start introducing new policies and technologies to improve your convenience. You can't do it overnight.

Marketing subsequent to the sale requires dedication and assiduous follow-up. But you can systematize your procedures in this important area, and it's a fairly easy habit to establish, especially when you see the payoff. Spotting the amazement in your business and then communicating it is also nice and straightforward. But engaging in measurement that helps you eliminate some marketing weapons while redoubling your efforts with others requires diligence of the highest order.

Guerrillas take pleasure when they intensify their involvement with customers. And they are quick to grasp the common sense of being more dependent upon others, seeking help from and giving help to a network of fellow guerrillas.

 ## The newest force in marketing

It seems appropriate within the context of this book that I add a thirteenth guerrilla marketing principle, another word that ends in "ent." It's *armament,* and it refers to technology. Armament is defined as the weapons, supplies, force, and equipment for war. I don't see marketing as war, but I do know that it is an ongoing battle for the mind, attention, and disposable income of your prospects. And I know that it will be won by the best prepared companies, using the most effective armament they can.

When these companies combine their weapons and supplies with a clear comprehension of what it takes to market a small business, they are formidable indeed. Technology is the newest force in marketing. Armed with it and the principles of marketing, small businesses can achieve huge victories.

 The people business

I reminded you at the beginning of this chapter that no matter what business your business card says you're in, you're really in the marketing business. Here, at the end of the chapter, I feel compelled to remind you that no matter what business you think you're in, you're also in the people business. People buy what you offer. People use what you offer. People benefit from what you offer. All of your customers will have at least one thing in common: they'll all be people.

Your ability to be a people person—to know that marketing that attracts and retains customers is really all about people—will dictate your success at gaining and satisfying customers. If you can do that, you're my kind of guerrilla.

chapter 4

⚔ The Business of Customers

Now that you know about marketing and have down pat the principles of attracting customers, it's time for you to fall in love with the notion of retaining those customers. And love is the right word.

Is running a business really like falling in love? It should be, if you're to be a guerrilla. I'm not talking about romantic love or even platonic love. I'm talking customer love. When you fall in love, you treat the one you love with eternal kindness, shower that person with attention, learn everything you can about the person, and do anything possible to make that person happy. You don't allow anything to get in the way of your relationship, because you want it to be long and cozy, and you want the object of your attention to feel loved.

Guerrillas are wonderful lovers. They allow their sensitivity and passion to fuel their relationships with customers. They sincerely care about those people, recognizing that each is special, each is unique, each is the real reason the business exists in the first place. Customers, like lovers, are treated with respect, honor, and reverence.

Customers actually sense your devotion. They know you care. In return, those customers bond to you, make you part of their identity, and speak of you only in the most glowing terms. They come back for more of what you offer. They are quick to sing your praises to others who might benefit from knowing you.

One-night stands and lasting relationships

Many small businesses treat sales transactions as one-night stands—fun while they last, but soon forgotten. Guerrillas treat sales transactions as the beginnings of beautiful and lasting relationships, which they nurture and help to flourish. To guerrillas, attracting customers is only half the job. The other half is retaining those customers. Where 46 percent of U.S. marketing budgets was invested in customer retention back in 1991, in 1996 that figure rose to 55 percent, and it's still growing.

In order to build lasting relationships with customers, you need insights into those customers that can come only from information. The more you know about your customers, the more you are able to make them happy, to surpass their expectations, to delight them. As it is better to know something about your spouse than to know everything about marriage, it is better to know something about your customers than to know everything about your business.

Being human

More and more small businesses are learning—often the hard way, by losing customers—that marketing isn't as much about being creative as it is about being human, about establishing and maintaining human connections, about treating customers the way they dream of being treated, not merely as they expect to be treated.

The key to unforgettable customer service is information. The more you know about each customer, the better you will be able to keep that customer happy. It's kind of ironic that the secret weapon for warm human relations is technology; but that's the case. Technology helps you collect information, stay in touch with customers, know what they like and don't like, communicate with them, and be there for them when they need you. It allows you to easily capture, store, organize, and analyze databases rich in information about each customer.

One guerrilla's database indicated that many of his customers owned Porsches. He learned this by sending questionnaires to his customers. A mailing to Porsche owners proved to be a bonanza. Another guerrilla learned from his database that an inordinate number of his customers watched reruns of *Star Trek*. He began running commercials during the show and broke the bank. Unlike Captain Kirk who boldly went where no man had gone before, this guy went exactly where his customers were going and found a galaxy of new customers waiting there.

 ## What technology is really about

Even though technology seems to be about machines, it's really about people. Technology allows you to maintain control of your relationships, saves time for you and your customers, and increases, your ability to please your customers. It enables you to lower your costs of pleasing customers while increasing your productivity, so that customers have more to be pleased about.

Because guerrillas know it costs six times more to sell something to a new customer than to sell the same thing to an existing customer, they excel at customer service. They know darned well that service is anything the customer wants it to be, and not just something written in a manual. Keeping customer satisfaction at the highest level isn't a sometime event; it's an all-the-time habit. And it applies to every customer.

Because guerrillas are spectacular listeners, they know what's on their customers' minds. They ask a lot of questions, often in the form of a customer questionnaire. And they enter

DEAR JAY,

How does a guerrilla in a larger organization calculate the value of the relationship-building techniques you speak about? Small businesses have regular and instant interaction with their customers and can implement your techniques without having to "sell it to the boss." When dollars and resources are limited in a larger corporate setting, marketing and public relations professionals are increasingly required to prove the value of these great techniques in terms of the bottom line. Creating an infrastructure to track and record the sales that result from the intangibles is difficult. How do you justify or explain the value of pursuing the love affair if your efforts don't result in immediate sales?
— Carole

DEAR CAROLE,

Relationships with customers are hard to quantify and translate into absolute profit figures, whether you're running a small or a big business. If people's eyes are always on the bottom line, they are focusing too narrowly. They should be concentrating on customer service and warm, close relationships, knowing that these do pay off on the bottom line in time.

Guerrillas have always known that to gain a share of market, they must first gain a share of mind. Caring service can gain that share for you. And while tracking sales that result from intangibles such as this is a grind, it can be accomplished with a follow-up questionnaire that allows people to tell you where and how they heard of you and why they did business with you.

Outstanding customer service rarely results in immediate sales, but it does result in eventual repeat and referral business, which is usually healthier than a single dose of instant sales. Guerrillas are famed for their patience, and always prefer rich, long-term rewards and a growing profit curve to the heady joy of fast bucks and a brief spike in their profits. — Jay

customers' answers into their database. The database teems, not only with names of customers, perhaps a business's most precious asset, but also with information about each customer.

 ## What guerrillas know

Guerrillas know what radio stations their customers listen to, which are their favorite TV shows, what newspapers they read, and to which magazines they subscribe. Guerrillas know how many kids their customers have, and even the names of the kids. They know where their customers went to college, what sports teams they support, their favorite charities, the kind of car they drive, how much money they earn, and lots of other details that are anything but small.

Do you know how guerrillas gain this crucial information? They ask for it. Sometimes it's through a questionnaire sent in the mail; sometimes the same questionnaire appears on their web site; sometimes it's e-mailed to customers; it can even be handed to customers in person at a store or trade show. The responses are studied carefully, and then action is taken based on what the guerrillas have learned.

That means they can send Christmas cards that say not only "Merry Christmas!" but also "Congratulations to your son for making the soccer team!" or "How about those Yankees?". They connect with personal references, making each customer feel singled out, recognized as the one-of-a-kind person that each of us really is. How often do you get greeting cards that feel so intensely personal? Not often. Perhaps not ever. And certainly not from a business. That's why, when you send them out, you'll be remembered.

Technology gives you a competitive edge when it comes to delighting customers, because it lets you talk to them about topics in which they have indicated an interest, meaningfully, thoughtfully, personally. It lets you have a dialogue with them. It lets you e-mail them when you know they'll be interested in what you have to say. It lets you answer all their questions by means of the online brochure at your customer-oriented web site. It lets you treat their requests with the speed they have learned to expect from you. It lets you render mind-boggling service.

 ## Customer bliss

As we come to the close of a century, it is no longer enough to strive for "customer satisfaction." The names of the game now are: customer delight, customer enchantment, and customer bliss.

Is intimacy too powerful a word? Not by any means. It is a word associated with lovers. The business of customers is learning to love them and knowing they will love you back, manifesting their love with repeat purchases, referral sales, and effusive testimonials. The motivation behind customer delight, customer enchantment, and customer bliss is a love of people, not a love of money.

 ## The consultant who charges no money

There's a first-rate consultant on customer bliss living in your home. It's you. You've been a customer for a long time, purchasing a broad range of products and services. You've been satisfied, dissatisfied, ripped off, treated well, ignored, catered to, fawned over, and high-pressured. How many times have you been delighted? What did the business do to delight you? If you made a list, it would be a very short one, because most businesses haven't a clue what it takes to surpass mere satisfaction.

It takes time. It takes energy. It takes attention. It takes data. It takes a deep-down caring attitude. It takes keeping track. It takes a mission statement dedicating yourself to surpassing satisfaction. If you've accomplished all of those and you'd like another competitive advantage, try surpassing customer satisfaction on a consistent basis.

Eye-to-Eye with Technology

After 30 years of solo practice, a Connecticut optometrist was seeing his business eroded by the national discount chains setting up shop in his community. By nature opposed to in-your-face advertising and promotion, he'd always assumed that the quality of his service would speak for itself, and that he'd always have a steady customer base. But when he started losing patients to the discounters he began to reconsider his aversion to marketing. Luckily, a patient running a marketing consulting business out of his home was available to lend his expertise, helping the optometrist evaluate how technology could help him compete for customers with the big guys without losing his personal touch.

They began by setting up a database of all patients. By studying the distribution of zip codes, they discovered that many patients seemed to be traveling significant distances from their homes. Further examination revealed that a large percentage of patients *worked* in the vicinity of the optometrist's office, and were visiting the optometrist as a matter of convenience. Armed with this information, the optometrist obtained a list of local businesses and launched a targeted fax campaign to attract new customers. Meanwhile, in an effort to retain existing customers, the marketing consultant used the database to sort names according to the date of the patient's last visit. To entice lapsed customers, the optometrist sent direct mail, offering a free lens upgrade through a cooperative advertising arrangement with the manufacturer.

Technology not only allowed the optometrist to learn more about his customers, but to reach them effectively through low-cost, low-pressure methods that were consistent with the style that sets him apart from the competition. His increased profits attest to the benefits of his increased use of technology.

 The hallmark of the twenty-first century

Developing relationships is all the rage in the enlightened nineties. Intensifying relationships will be the hallmark of the twenty-first century. Growing closer to customers by means of contact will motivate them to grow closer to you. The connection between you and your customers grows stronger with regular newsletters, letters, postcards, phone calls, e-mails, and faxes. You build on the rapport you established at the very start of the relationship. And always, you know the difference between doing it and overdoing it.

Guerrillas know well that their customers are their best sales force. They are nearly obsessed with wondering what

Dear Jay,

I have been in the computer business for 25 years. About 15 years ago, my manager at the time was analyzing the different types of people on the sales force. Some he described as Technical Sales People (able to talk the language of the systems engineers) and others as Numbers Sales People (those who make twice as many calls a day because they hope that statistically more calls will mean more "hits"). Then he said, "Mike, you're something else again. You are a 'Rapport Salesman.' You understand all of the facets of a customer from technical to financial to the fact that they invite you to their parties." I considered and consider this to be one of the proudest moments of my career.

However, recently I interviewed for a position with a relatively new start-up company, and when asked what my philosophy was, I responded with everything you state in this chapter (not using the "lover" metaphor, however!). The next day I was contacted by the recruiter who told me I hadn't gotten the job because they considered me "old-fashioned" in my approach to sales. How do you reconcile your philosophy with the movement of nearly every product and service toward "commoditization," decreasing prices, and "volume sales?" Why would customers do business with someone they like when they can go to an impersonal discount chain and acquire the same products for so much less? Does the lover/rapport approach only work in certain markets? — Mike

they might do for their customers that the customers would never expect. They offer their customers: a toll-free hotline; a web site; after-hours telephone answering capability. They give their customers: free tip sheets; free items with orders to say "thank you"; free shipping as a surprise extra; discount coupons for new products or services; free access to their

---

DEAR MIKE,

I applaud you for being a rapport salesman and feel that this ability will help you sell almost anything to anybody. The idea of building rapport is both old-fashioned and new wave, and it's the key to the success of many who are engaged in sales. Any business that feels rapport-building is too old-fashioned sounds like a business with the wrong chemistry for you.

Although some companies are moving toward lower prices and higher volume, more are moving toward establishing warm and lasting relationships with their customers. In fact, no product category in America is led by the lowest-priced brand. And sales of high-ticket items are growing at a much faster rate than sales of low-price items.

The reason to do business the way you do is to enjoy your work while enjoying your life. Connections such as those you make with your customers lead to long-term relationships, repeat business, and referral business. Connections based on impersonal items such as price are often one-shot deals with very little, if any, loyalty.

The rapport approach works in most businesses, and because you are able to establish it well I hope you look for work in firms that will appreciate your ability to get close to customers. Your talent is rare. I hope you use it and put it to work for one of the many companies that will appreciate it. — Jay

business library; tours of their business; free consultations; free delivery; free installation; free repairs; free snacks or coffee while they're visiting. In the name of superb service they offer extended hours of business, a guarantee on everything they sell, referrals to the customer's business, and more. Most of all, they listen to customers, then act upon what they've heard. They never fail to keep their promises.

If you're going to be a guerrilla, you're going to invest time, energy, and imagination, as well as money, in attracting customers. Actually you'll be attracting prospects, then, if you're good at what you do, you'll convert them into customers. Oh happy day—right? Not right—if you don't also invest time, energy, imagination, and money in retaining those customers. If you do the former and not the latter, all your investments in attracting and converting customers will be down the tube.

 ## Statistics to make you frown

If you think that's bad news, it's almost good news compared with these statistics, supplied by the White House Office of Consumer Affairs:

- 96 percent of unhappy customers will never complain about shabby service from you, but you won't see 90 percent of them again.

- Each of your unhappy customers will tell their sad tale to at least 9 other people, and 18 percent of those will say bad things behind your back to 22 people.

Outstanding customer service has to start at the very beginning, with your very first customer. This objective must be very clear in your mind and your mission. You've got to hire or connect with people who have a sincere attitude of caring and wanting to render service. If you hire meanies and train them, you won't have true rapport builders working for you but only a bunch of trained meanies.

The big deterrent

Not surprisingly, one of the biggest deterrents to spectacular customer service is spectacular growth. Businesses add so many new customers that they become addicted to growth and focus on adding more customers rather than taking exceptional care of the ones they have. Like shooting heroin, they get a short-term kick but are in for long-term misery. One by one, their new customers desert them for the competition. Many companies have a plan in case of failure, but very few have a plan in case of success. Guerrillas know just how to succeed, and they know it means treating all customers with care and attention. They know customers leave not just because of poor or rude service, but mainly because they are just plain ignored.

Does this mean all customers should be treated exactly the same? It does not. It means that all customers should be revered, but some should be treated with more reverence than others.

A lists and B lists

Guerrilla businesses divide their customers into at least two categories: their A list, made up of customers who buy the most, spend the most, are the nicest, and refer the most; and their B list, made up of all other customers. Those on the B list are showered with attention, contact, and special favors. Those on the A list are showered with even more attention, contact, and special favors. Guerrillas are very quick to play favorites. They know that 80 percent of their business comes from 20 percent of their customers, and that they should devote 80 percent of their service energy toward those 20 percent.

These guerrillas are also acutely aware that technology allows them to communicate one-on-one with their customers, so that high-tech results in high-touch. One-on-one is the very essence of interactive marketing. It refers to in-person meetings, telephone contact, personal (not merely personalized) letters, personal (never mass) e-mail, and a database that is updated regularly because customers change regularly. It is the very opposite of mass marketing. And it's a boon to small business.

Keeping customers by keeping track

Technology allows guerrillas to keep track of all their contacts with customers so that they don't have to rely solely upon their memories. It lets them concentrate on crucial, super-powered details such as their customers' birthdays, anniver-

DEAR JAY,
We recently had a state government agency award our company a contract to install a statewide LAN-WAN network, plus desktop PCs, servers, and notebook PCs. We are a "virtual office" of three people. The project succeeded: on-time, full-function, and within budget. So what's the problem?

We practice, and therefore support strongly, your prescription for intimacy and involvement with the customer. However, the customer returned that feeling and started involving us in "opportunities" outside of our business focus. We have the expertise to satisfy most of these opportunities. But we planned on adding more customers, rather than broadening our focus. Since we want to please the customer, and adhere to our business plan, and don't have the staff to do both, what guidelines can you suggest for evaluating alternatives and making a decision(s)?
— Christine, Jim, and Tony

saries, promotions at work, interests, past purchases, and—especially—their problems. This gives small business owners the opportunity to gain a competitive edge by tailoring their service to the needs of their customers. It gives them the share of mind that is so necessary if they're to obtain the share of market they want.

Although technology as a customer service tool is relatively new, it has won the hearts of small business owners across America. A full 82 percent of them say they have confidence in the payoff of new technologies. The majority of these business owners, 66 percent, feel that the biggest payoff will be in the area of customer service, while 64 percent figure it will be in marketing.

~~~~~~~~~~~~~~~~~~~~~~~~~~~~~~~~~

DEAR CHRISTINE, JIM, AND TONY,
First, I highly recommend that you read Al Ries's dynamite book, Focus, *in which he relates many horror stories of firms that suffered disasters when they lost their focus. As much as I counsel small businesses to render superlative service, I counsel them even stronger to maintain their focus. And that's exactly what I'm suggesting to you. Explain to your customer that you'll be a much more effective company if you remain focused. Then do everything you can to locate a firm that can help your customer accomplish what they wish.*
Aligning yourself with some good subcontractors is a good idea, because you can get project management fees, keep the customer happy, and still achieve your goal of adding more customers within your area of expertise. If you do this, you'll be succeeding at both service and focus. It's a neat problem you have and I congratulate you on realizing that your focus should be foremost. — Jay

~~~~~~~~~~~~~~~~~~~~~~~~~~~~~~~~~

Two things to learn

You've got to learn two things if you're to become a customer service superstar:

1. Which of the new technologies do your customers use?

2. Which of the new technologies do your competitors use?

Then, because you're a guerrilla, you act upon what you learn. You employ the technologies used by your customers. If they aren't online yet, your e-mail capability will have to wait till they are, and you must focus upon your other technology. If your competitors offer data by fax and you don't, you're operating out of a hole. The idea is to meet your customers' technological standards and to surpass those of your competitors.

Be prepared to open your mind to a host of technologies that I haven't even delved into here: teleconferencing, video conferencing, satellite transmission, online coupons, interactive kiosks, multimedia presentations, brochures on computer disks, CD-ROMs, networks, and customer hotlines. The list goes on, and all you've got to do is read the daily newspaper to see new technologies unveiled that can make the difference between red and black on your bottom line.

If you've got a web site that is self-contained or that offers few links to others, you're robbing yourself of the co-marketing opportunities now available on the Internet, and robbing your customers of information that would help them. Freely giving information of value to your customers is part of superb customer service. Don't shortchange these important people in this area.

 ## The changing customer

There are a myriad of new technologies to empower your customer service. But it will be empowered the most when you

Adventures in Technology

Perhaps the last place you'd expect to find sophisticated computerized operations is at a touring concessionaire in the Southwest that sends jeep-riding adventurers into the rugged terrain. With its "mission to sell fun," the outfitter, with a fleet of 30 vehicles, launches 45 to 50 tours a day. The company is equipped to send 60,000 passengers out in a year. The trick, of course, is to run at full capacity, loading the jeeps efficiently and keeping track of all vehicles, guides, and passenger reservations to ensure a smooth turnover of equipment and customers.

Traditionally the company had relied on a color-coded magnetic board to track guides and jeeps. But the margin for error was high and the system was not fully integrated with reservations and customer traffic control, leading to bottlenecks and duplicative efforts. A PC server–based system with database management tools

has taken the guesswork out of traffic management. Using this technology, the company duplicated its magnetic scheduling board electronically, preserving the format but eliminating errors and allowing for accurate, real-time updates to track the location and capacity of all vehicles. The system provides the flexibility to take, manage, and change reservations at a moment's notice; as customer traffic flow is managed proactively, jeeps and guides can be monitored to meet demand exactly.

The results: with no scrambling to find drivers, no overbooking, and no long waits, the company projects an image of confidence and professional service to its customers; happy customers, in turn, boost company morale and provide incentives to grow the business. An added bonus is the good rapport that has been established with the National Forest Service as a result of the company's reputation for carefully documenting activity on park land.

recognize the change in customers. They recognize the difference between satisfactory and exceptional service. They understand that technology can help you help them. They are more demanding, less easily satisfied, increasingly sophisticated, and able to switch allegiances in a flash. These insights into the changing customer put a smile on the face of a guerrilla, because he or she knows very well that these new truths represent a glorious opportunity to stand out in the customer service arena.

You must know the difference between doing things right the first time and doing things over. And you must never forget that at all times you're in three different businesses: your business, the marketing business, and the people business. Unless you excel at all three, you run the risk of going out of business.

chapter 5

Zero to 60 in 30 Days

When I write a book, I always figure that it's a two-part process: starting the book, which takes only one page, and finishing the book, which takes another 200 or so pages. But getting started seems to be half the job, because when I'm ready to start it means I know what I'll be doing and I'm prepared to forge ahead.

To my way of thinking, the same is true of using technology in your business. Getting started is half the battle. In order to start, you must feel confident, informed, in complete control, and motivated by the benefits of technology—increased productivity, inventory control, better customer service, new revenue opportunities, a more professional identity, and greater speed.

The wrong reason to use technology

It's not a good idea to use technology just because you think you should. Instead, use it to accomplish specific goals. For instance, I used to write direct mail letters for a bank. I'd use my typewriter. Often the letters would be mailed to ten different groups for testing. Each letter would be the same except for one paragraph. It was a major pain for me to type each letter, so I considered buying a word processor because I knew that with this tool I could write one letter, then easily change the paragraphs without needing to start from scratch. In addition, I am a very fast typist and I resented the need to keep hitting the carriage return on my typewriter, something I wouldn't have to do with a word processor. Those two factors got me started in technology.

Soon afterward, I realized that I could save trips to and from my client's office if I purchased a fax machine, which I did. And later, when I teamed up with an author on the East Coast to write a book, I quickly learned the beauty and benefits of e-mail and being online. My journey into technology started with those needs to save time, and once I embraced the technology, there was no looking back.

Right now you may be poised on the threshold of using technology to add teeth to your marketing or to save valuable time for yourself. Perhaps you have some other ideas in mind for how high tech can translate into high profits. But before you dive into the pool, you want to make sure it's filled with water. So where do you dip your toes? Do you look first to your needs? To the capabilities of technology? To your budget? Right, right, and right. You're asking the right questions, thinking the right thoughts.

 ## High tech and high stress

I know that high tech means high anxiety to many people, but I also know that their stress is based upon complicated older technology and not upon the simple technology of today. It's this high anxiety that keeps many entrepreneurs away from just what they need the most. A survey of small business owners in 1997 revealed that nearly 20 percent of them feel that lack of knowledge kept them from buying more technology, yet 40 percent said that technology is critical to their business success.

If you're planning to use technology to send your profits soaring, there's a ten-step plan to follow. Before you even begin to institute this plan, recognize that you will succeed with technology, as with marketing, if you decide up front that you're going to commit to it, stick with it, and make it work for you no matter what. Then it's time to activate the plan. Once you do, you will wonder why you waited.

A ten-step plan

Suppose you've got a small retail store, the Ashby Design Shop, in a city of 100,000. You've been running your store for over a decade and sales seem to have plateaued, though you work full-bore to keep the competition at bay. Your products are mattresses and bedding. You've experimented with many other furniture items but learned that mattresses are your bread and butter. How will this ten-step plan apply to you?

step 1   **Engage in research**   Find out what others in your industry are using for marketing, merchandising, and production. Find out what's available, what you can afford, and what's coming up next. The idea is to begin operating from a standpoint of knowledge instead of ignorance. Keep your radar attuned to which technology will improve your effectiveness and your efficiency, which can light a fire under your marketing, which can save your time and money, and which can add luster to your customer service.

The Ashby Design Shop's research turned up three ways that technology could provide competitive strengths and advantages. One was a computer and software that would enable the shop to create its own marketing materials, especially monthly flyers that could be distributed through fusion marketing partners and posted as signs on bulletin boards in the community. Another was a marketing-on-hold telephone system that would allow callers to hear news of special prices and products while on hold.

The third was an innovative computer that measured pressure points on a body lying on a mattress. The Ashby Design Shop manufactured several mattresses that were demonstrably superior with regard to pressure points, and the computer allowed customers to see this superiority in front of them on a color monitor at the same time as they felt it while lying on the mattress itself.

step **2** **Check out your competitors** The last thing you want is for them to offer more convenience and better service than you, so see what they're up to. Learn how technology is helping them. The idea isn't to catch up to them but to surpass them.

The owner of the Ashby Design Shop took two major trips strictly to check up on retailers in the same business as him. Although his store was in Berkeley, California, he shopped at mattress stores in Los Angeles, Denver, Chicago, New York, Atlanta, London, Paris, Copenhagen, and Amsterdam looking for good ideas embracing technology. I realize this isn't typical, but his wife was his partner on these spying sojourns, and so a reconnaissance mission was combined with a vacation. They learned of a new construction technology that was not available in the U.S., and as a result established a fusion business arrangement with the Scandinavian manufacturer.

step **3** **Check your own customers** What technologies do your customers use? If they're still using fax machines and aren't yet online, perhaps you don't have to be online either. But if they're using the web and know where to look for things there, you'd better get yourself a web site pronto. Again, your job is not just to keep up with your customers but to stay ahead of them, offering the ultimate in convenience to both customers and prospects.

The Ashby Design Shop mailed a brief questionnaire to its customer list and learned that the shop should get online immediately, because over half of the shop's customers were already quite familiar with e-mail, the web, and the Internet, where they were finding much information—and many of the shop's competitors. Because the Ashby Design Shop has always been sensitive to the needs of its customers, the owner now has created a web site, responds to e-mail daily, and is already discovering the benefits of linking to other businesses in the community—some, naturally, run by the shop's customers.

Today the shop has a regular monthly e-mailing to customers who have requested it. I suppose the term for this might be follow-up-on-demand.

step 4 **Limit your purchases to your real needs** Once you have determined those needs, you'll know which technology to purchase and which you can do without for the time being. There's no need to arm yourself to fight a tiger when all you'll be facing is a pussycat. On the other hand, you don't want to be prepared only for pussycats when you're being charged by tigers. The key is to fortify yourself with the appropriate technology to serve your own needs. A consultant might be just the ticket to help you in this area.

The Ashby Design Shop wanted to be able to print oversize color point-of-purchase signs, but the owner settled on buying only the software for the job because he learned he could farm out the color printing to Kinko's.

step 5 **Examine your alternatives** Here I am praising computers and technology to the skies when I well know that computers aren't the solution to every problem and that advanced voice mail systems can lose customers for you as easily as they can gain them. Picasso once said that the problem with computers is that all they can do is come up with the right answers, but not the right questions. It's up to you to ask those right questions. How can you improve your customer service with technology? How can you add more effectiveness to your marketing with technology? How can you streamline your way of doing business with technology? If you ask those kinds of questions you'll be able to use technology to provide the answers. Where computers used to be a luxury to small business, each day they're becoming more of a necessity. Operating a business without them today is like operating a business 50 years ago without a telephone.

When the Ashby Design Shop decided to invest in the computer that shows pressure points where a body touches a mattress, it was venturing into new territory, trying to come up with a competitive edge that would be meaningful and dramatic. It was asking what it takes to convince a person that one mattress is better than another. Because the public is learning more and more to trust technology, the design shop decided to use a technical device as a marketing tool, and then another technical device—the computer used to create flyers and signs—to produce marketing weapons promoting that tool.

step **6** **Talk to your staff** Don't keep it a secret. Your task is to get them to want the technology as much as you do, to embrace it with the same enthusiasm as you. Many of today's computer whizzes were scared to death to touch a keyboard or click a mouse just a few years ago. So take the time to get feedback from your people, to enlist their aid, to make them feel part of the move to technology rather than like they are being brushed aside by it. Their comfort level with technology is every bit as important as yours. The last thing you want is the right technology being ignored by a staff that's terrified of it. If they're involved up front, they'll stay involved.

The proprietor of the Ashby Design Shop discussed his foray into technology with his staff, soliciting opinions and advice as he went along. Some of his younger employees were more computer literate than he was, so they illuminated the path for him. The entire staff enjoyed their involvement in selecting the technology they were going to employ, and fully understood the reason for each investment.

step **7** **Develop a plan and put it in writing** Just as guerrillas have a written marketing plan, they have a written technology plan which lays out which technologies they'll need and when they'll need them. After you've completed the preceding steps, write your plan. You probably won't want to purchase all your equipment at the same time, but which will you need first? Second? Third? Get those priorities straight, then live up to your plan. You'll find that the plan simplifies both the purchasing and the mastery of your equipment.

The owner of the Ashby Design Shop could not formulate his plan at the outset, as he would have with most plans. A technology plan is different. He had to learn before he could draft his plan. Research had to precede everything. He had to know where his competitors and customers fit on the technology spectrum before he could engage in intelligent planning. He had to be aware of his needs before he planned to fill them. And he had to attempt a smooth confluence between his staff and the technology, never forcing one upon the other.

step **8** **Train your staff** If you can't do it yourself, or if an articulate employee can't do it, bring in a trainer or a tutor who can show your staff the ropes and the simplicity of your technology. You want your people to look forward to using it, to use it with aplomb, and never to resent it. If they feel they are in control of the technology instead of the reverse, you're off to a splendid start.

The Ashby Design Shop owner took the training himself in a two-day course, then trained his staff. Two were taught to use the computer to create flyers and to operate the marketing-on-hold telephone system, while all employees were trained how to use the computer to close sales and how to use the pressure-point computer to demonstrate mattresses.

step **9** **Purchase equipment you can grow into, not out of** The first thing you want is a computer with enough power to run all the software you'll be using. The last thing you want is to need even more power later because you've grown so successful. Don't sacrifice quality in this area. Be willing to fork out enough to a top-quality vendor for top-quality technology. Maybe it's more power and more technology than you need right now, but you'll be much happier growing into it than realizing you'll soon outgrow it.

Whatever you purchase will be improved, and the price will drop, within a few months. That's the nature of the technology beast. But never forget that you can upgrade if you have to. Software keeps getting better and easier to use, and it's very simple to merely upgrade your software without having to purchase a new or more powerful computer. A small business is like a new family; it doesn't make sense to purchase a one-bedroom house with a baby on the way and a few more planned for later. A three-bedroom house may be a bit too large at first, but you can grow into it and won't have

Dear Jay,
How do you keep up with the increasing pace of technology? — Art

Dear Art,
Technological change is an inevitable event, like death and taxes. There's no sense worrying about whether or not your hardware will become obsolete or your software will be enhanced with new and better features than the version you have today: it will. So the best thing to do to keep up is to focus not on the products themselves but on what the ever-advancing technologies allow you to do. Could you market your business better by upgrading your technology? Is there a way to stay in better touch with customers? Could you reduce your paperwork? Identify your issues, seek out news and advice on only those technologies that get you where you want to go, and ignore the rest until they're relevant to you. There is a wealth of sources in print, on TV and radio, and, of course, on the Internet, that can help. Whatever you do, keep up-to-date. After all, you don't want your competitors to beat you to the punch and win customers who should be yours.

As for me, keeping up on technology is an ongoing adventure: I read several magazines each week, read at least two books about technology each month, watch TV shows about technology, and rely upon several friends who are light years ahead of me in the techno-world for their expertise and their cautions. I ask questions, learn from their mistakes, and benefit from their wise moves. — Jay

to start looking for a new house when you should be settling into one.

It was quite a leap for the Ashby Design Shop to go from zero technology—not even a customer database—to a powerful computer, a database teeming with information about each customer, a regular program of marketing using computer-generated materials, a warm and friendly marketing-on-hold system, and a hybrid computerized mattress pressure point tester. Those items are in place now, and both sales and profits are the highest they've been in the history of the Ashby Design Shop. There is more store traffic due to the flyers and signs. The close ratio is far better due to the computerized mattress tester. All the technology paid for itself in 15 months. And the same technology continues to satisfy the demands of the business. It's not always such a sweet story, but it can be.

step 10 **Evaluate your progress** At the end of each month, check to see if you're following your plan, if your technology is serving all your needs, if your staff is comfortable with the technology, if your customers are happy. Settle for nothing less than complete satisfaction. Is the technology doing exactly what you wanted it to do? If not, make changes so that it does.

The Ashby Design Shop is now focusing on improving traffic and on responses it gets from its web site in an effort to convert visitors into customers. It's trying to find more links and more fusion marketing partners. After being skittish about technology during his first ten years in business, the owner now has his nose buried in reading *The Internet for Dummies,* and you can't be in his showroom for more than five minutes without somebody pointing out the computer that tests mattress pressure points, which looks as though it came right from *Star Wars.* He moved into the world of technology slowly, but now that he's in it, he'll never return to the old way of doing business. He took ten steps and they led him into his future.

By getting started this way, you'll find that you can be up and running, benefiting from the immense power of technology, in a month or less. All the steps I've outlined above can be accomplished within a period of 30 days, except for the evaluation part, which should be a continuing process.

 ## More than you bargained for

As I mentioned, I invested in my computer strictly for word processing. But yesterday I used it for e-mail, chatting with a friend in London, accessing sports scores, playing a trivia game, downloading medical information from the Net, and listening to my newest CD. Not one bit of word processing. You'll also discover that technology can do a whole lot more for you than you could ever have guessed before you started putting it to use for yourself.

It's very important that you become involved not with the technology itself, which can be ultra-fascinating, but with what the technology can do for you. All the bells and whistles in the world won't increase your profitability if it can't delight your customers and satisfy their specific needs. Never forget that your customers should be the beneficiaries of your leap into the techno-world, and that advanced technology is all about them, not about you. If you keep that fact at the forefront of your mind, you'll stay on the right track.

When purchasing software, it's always a good idea to test it yourself. You can begin at the software company's web site and check their demonstration programs to be sure they're compatible with your needs.

 ## The human factor

Never forget that technology is merely a tool and that you are the person who will be using it. That means making certain you'll be physically comfortable when using it. Take heed of the light in your office, the comfort of your chair. Make sure your monitor is at eye level and that you use a keyboard that is ergonomically correct. The more natural your position while you're working, the better. Technology may seem to be all about machines, but it's very much about people too.

The cost of technology

When you purchase a car or a new piece of furniture, it's an expense, and it's probably going to be worth your money. When you purchase technology for your business, it is an expense also. But it's even more of an investment, because it will be able to contribute mightily to your profitability. Unlike Wall Street investments, your technology investment poses little risk if you operate according to the ten-step plan I've just outlined. You're in control of this investment. You have the opportunity to maximize the returns it can deliver by your wise use of its capabilities.

By availing yourself of the extraordinary new phenomenon of the Internet, you can establish strategic alliances and engage in global commerce while marketing inexpensively and powerfully, not to mention interactively. The mind-boggling capacity to do this is brought within reach by today's simple technology, which unleashes creative forces within you that may never have been tapped before.

When to begin

There are wrong times and right times to begin to enlist the aid of technology in your business. The wrong times are after you've waited for prices to drop, after you've waited for computer power to increase, and after your competitors have already wooed away your customers. The right times are ten years ago and immediately.

Be ready to upgrade your technology when necessary, and never fail to know the difference between change for its own sake and change for the purpose of improvement. You— and your customers—want the latter. These days, if you're not staying ahead of the game, you're probably losing it.

chapter 6

Saving Money by Saving Time

I've never written a chapter of a book that started out with a lie. But I'm going to do it now. Not only will I tell you a lie, but I'll tell you a dirty lie, one that is hurtful to your business and your associates, to your family and yourself. Worst of all, it's a lie that you've probably been buying into most of your life.

Here it is: Time is money.

Don't believe it.

Don't believe it for one instant. Time is far more valuable than money. Run out of money and you'll probably find ways to scrounge up some more. Run out of time and that's the end of the ride. No way to get any more. Time, instead of being money, is life itself.

You can use time to earn more money, to be sure. You can use it to polish your business, grow your business, maximize your business, and amass awesome profits. You can also use it to add balance to your life by pursuing leisure activities, being with your friends and family, or just chilling out. The key idea isn't necessarily what you do with your time, but that now you can get more of it than ever before with the proper mindset and by availing yourself of the myriad of new technologies designed with the underlying prime benefit of saving enormous chunks of time for you. That's really what computers are all about: speed and saving time.

Guerrillas and time

Guerrillas cherish their time, use it wisely, and, like most Americans, now consider time to be their most precious asset. They know that time isn't money, that it's considerably more valuable than money, and that technology can bestow more of it to them now than at any time in history.

Guerrillas also follow a five-step time-saving plan created solely to free up more of their time. It's a plan that can do the same for you. Your business plan will generate growth for you. Your marketing plan will generate profits for you. Your technology plan will help you to improve those profits. Your time-saving plan will generate extra time for you.

 ## A five-step time-saving plan

As you don't have to learn the names of your digestive enzymes to enjoy a hearty meal, you won't have to learn the jargon of technology to enjoy the time-saving benefits it bestows. All you've really got to learn is: how you are spending your time now; how you should be spending your time; where you can save time; how to save time in the areas you've identified; and whether the technologies you're embracing are truly saving your time. When you know those things, you'll be well on your way to having more time to devote to any pursuits you desire.

Before you even start developing your plan, you've got to begin with a powerful commitment to save time. As the trick to successful marketing is commitment to a plan with the goal of earning profits, the starting point to successful time-saving is a commitment to a plan with the goal of saving time. Without your commitment, it's not going to happen. With commitment, you just can't miss.

That commitment will embrace both the right ways to think about time and the right ways to use and save time. Yes, the plan will also save you money. Yes, it will fuel your profits. But remember that its prime purpose is to save you time. Once you have that time, it's yours to use any way you'd like.

step **1** **How you spend your time now**   Take a full two weeks to keep a daily log of your activities at work, writing down what you do and how much time it is taking you to do it. Write down each task you perform, regardless of how insignificant it may seem. Your employees and associates should be encouraged to do the same, because you want an overview of how all time is spent by your company. By reviewing the log at the end of the two weeks, you'll have a pretty good fix on how you're spending your time at work.

My guess is that you're going to be surprised when you see how much time you're devoting to your tasks. And you won't need me to point out which of those tasks should be completed by someone other than you. But be careful not to assume that just because someone else is assigned a task it will be done more efficiently. If you are spending hours filling out purchase orders by hand, it doesn't really save your company time or money to have someone else do the task by hand. Determine which tasks can best be handled by technology and which tasks are taking up more time than you or your company ought to be devoting to them.

step **2** **How you should spend your time**   Spend one hour or less making a list of the things you should be doing to make your company flourish and prosper. That includes a whole lot more than putting out fires to maintain the status quo. It also means doing what must be done to service existing customers, attract new customers, streamline your procedures, and improve your offerings. If you spend your time the way you think you should be spending it, you'll be operating in a growth mode rather than merely treading water.

This step will help you to determine the difference between efficiency, which is doing things right, and effectiveness, which is doing the right things. Guerrillas never choose between the two, but embrace both. They want to spend their time doing the right things the right way. And they want to do them right the first time. Accomplishing a task rapidly but having to do it again is both inefficient and ineffective.

step **3** **Where you can save time**   Examine every single aspect of the way you are doing business and put into writing those activities in which you can save time by doing them another way. Perhaps you'll save a lot of time by delegating, since guerrillas rarely do what they can delegate; they save themselves for the more important tasks of marketing aggressively and servicing assiduously. Possibly you will see areas in which technology can come to your aid in the quest for more time. Consider chores such as getting, sorting, opening, and reading the mail. Consider routine correspondence and paying bills. Consider billing and collecting, accounting, and data entry.

Also, be aware of whether you're a morning person or one who thrives when burning the midnight oil. If you know your own prime time, you'll be able to schedule your activities to match your energy level, and you'll complete more work in less time.

step **4** **How you will save time**   Here's where you make concrete decisions as to what you'll do to save time. For example, this is where you decide to put up your own web site to market your offerings twenty-four hours a day, seven days a week. If your presentations can be standardized so each one isn't a major time-consuming project, this is where you invest in the equipment to do that task. This is where you select the hardware and software to serve your specific needs. You can't really ask someone to recommend a specific computer to you, because that's like asking someone to recommend a religion. But experts can recommend software to speed you on the path to your goals, and I guarantee that the technology is out there to help you.

Will a voice mail system save time for you? Fax on demand? Marketing-on-hold telephone? Automatic reminders for customer follow-up? A database that organizes your inventory and a network system that allows others to have access to the information? A contact management software package that organizes your clients, your vendors, and your day? This is the step where you put your money where your commitment is—in the technology that will save time for you.

step **5** **Keeping track of your time-saving**   This final step means that you once again should keep a log for two

Making Business As Easy As Pie

As a Blacksburg, Virginia, bakery grew into a full-service retailer, wholesaler, and caterer, its owner—a chemist by training—recognized the inadequacy of the company's manual operating, reporting, and information systems. What worked with six employees and a few good recipes no longer worked with 23 employees and a portfolio of breads, pastries, pies, cakes, and lunch and catering menus. Frustration grew as owner and employees alike were buried under mountains of paperwork for every order, delivery, or shipment.

Initially reluctant to give up hands-on control of functions to a machine, the owner finally took the technology plunge, investing modestly in a system that could provide word processing, financial analysis, and database capabilities. The impact has been enormous. Having discarded her cumbersome ledger, the owner can now analyze financials at a glance and react quickly to head off problems or anticipate business trends. Marketing is a snap: instead of sending materials out to an ad agency (at $200 a pop) and then to the local copy shop, the bakery now produces its own flyers, signs, menus, and shipping labels. The database allows the company to identify delinquent accounts and bill customers more efficiently, improving cash flow. Despite the owner's trepidation, the computer system has, in fact, allowed her and her staff to take greater control of the business and of the time they spend at work, freeing resources for more productive activity during the day (with direct bottom-line results) and providing a greater balance for the entire staff between work and home life.

weeks of how you're spending your time now that your technology is up and running. If you've gone about things in the right way, you're getting more done and you're spending less time doing it. You're doing a better job of staying in touch with your current customers and you're putting out the word all over the place to obtain new ones. Your web site is humming and preselling your offerings, possibly even consummating many sales. Your flyers and newsletters, direct mailings, and proposals have twice the sparkle they used to while taking less than half the time to prepare.

Technology is helping you work faster, get more accomplished, establish closer relationships, and save time to capitalize on opportunities you might have missed because of lack of time. Even after the two weeks have passed you should constantly track your time, because you'll always find areas in which to improve, ways to save time, methods of growing your business.

 ## More time than you think

Even if you conscientiously follow this five-step time-saving plan, you still may discover that technology can save you time in even more areas than you imagined. I bought my first computer exclusively for word processing, knowing that would save me loads of writing time, typing time, and editing time. Little did I realize that it would save me even more time by granting me access to the Internet. Writing books for me used to mean frequent trips to the library. Now it means clicking my mouse and visiting the information superlibrary—the Net. The information is better and the time taken to collect it is a fraction of what it used to be.

I never dreamt that e-mail would prove so efficient and time-saving for communications. I didn't have an inkling of the time I'd save publishing marketing materials on my own. How long do you think it used to take me to mail three thousand brief letters compared to the time it takes now that I can do it with the click of a mouse? It's rare when I crunch numbers, but when I do my computer does for me in one minute what used to take five hours. I was always pretty good at keeping records, but I was operating in the Dark Ages before I got my computer. It's easier, faster, and more fun now than ever, and I didn't even realize I was operating in slow motion until I got the perspective I have now. At first I laughed at how mired I used to be, and then I winced when I thought of the missed opportunities.

I figured my computer would save time for me. I had no idea it would enable me to accomplish twice as much work, earn twice as much money, and put in half the time that I used to. As its primary gift to me, technology gave me time. As its secondary gift, it gave me even more time. I use it to write two books a year, not just one, because I can collaborate with coauthors from anywhere. Recently I entered into an arrangement with a man from Japan to coauthor a book about maintaining business efficiency while traveling, a book for mobile guerrillas. We'll join literary forces by e-mail and probably won't meet till the book has been published, if we meet at all. The networking opportunities of technology alone are gems of time-savers.

 ## Ten tips for organizing your business to save time

Although technology can save you more time than any other business strategy, followed closely by wise delegation of duties, simply being organized can also save you time and money. Of the countless ways of helping you get organized, here are ten to set you on your way:

1. Make sure everything in your office is business-related. Those things that aren't helping you stay in business may gang up to put you out of business. They are time bandits that rob you of precious time. If your home phone rings in your office, your work time is being stolen from you.

2. Take control of your time by means of a daily calendar containing your "to do" list. You can do it on paper or electronically, just as long as you do it. And once you've made that "to do" list, assign a priority to each task so that you complete the important ones first.

3. Set up your office so that you can reach anything you need in just seconds. Keep your phone, fax, computer, printer, and other equipment on a table of their own, within arm's reach, so that your desk is free for your paperwork.

4. Use a phone log or contact management program to enter phone numbers and messages. That way you'll know just where to look when you have to get in touch with somebody. You'd be floored if you knew how much time it takes to find phone numbers jotted down on scraps of paper. Even if it takes only one minute, when you multiply that minute by the times you spend hunting for each number, it adds up to hours.

5. Store all your paperwork vertically instead of horizontally. This will save time as well as space. Stacks of paper are a sure sign of disorganization. Efficiency experts tell us that the typical American executive wastes an average of three hours a week searching for lost or misplaced documents. That's nearly a full week out of every year.

6. When paperwork comes to you, handle it, and move it forward. Perhaps you'll toss it. Maybe you'll add its tasks to your "to-do" list. Possibly you'll forward it to someone else. The important thing is to handle it one time only.

7. Keep your files skinny. Most of the papers in your files just take up space and waste your time as you look for others. It's healthy to be slim whether you're a person or a file.

8. Put everything in its own place. Haphazard stashing is the bane of many small businesses. Guerrillas may have many business-related items in their office, but they know where to find them in an instant. The average business executive has 36 hours of work on his or her desk at any given time—far more than he or she can ever hope to accomplish in a workday. Having these documents in full view reminds the executive of what he or she can't accomplish, creating undue pressure and prompting him or her to tackle projects randomly rather than by priority.

9. At the end of each day, plan the next day. This will let you start the day running. Streamlined business owners enter their office in the morning to find a clean desktop and a prioritized "to do" list. They don't waste valuable time figuring out what to do next; they already know.

10. Place a high value on yourself. If you value yourself, you'll value your time. You'll know when you're working at your peak and sculpt your work flow to take advantage of that period. At the same time, place a high value on your technologies and learn to maximize their effectiveness. Most small business owners are getting a mere fraction of the value their technology offers. This includes your word processor, spreadsheet, database, and information management systems. And it also includes your familiarity with the Internet.

Once you're on the road to saving time, keep in mind that the time you save should not be used in drudgery but in productivity. The question that guerrillas ask is: "What is the best use of my time right now?" Their answer is never "I don't know." Instead, because they've organized their priorities and identified their goals, it's always very obvious to them what to do next.

 ## Being aware of time bandits

Even if you're committed to saving time, you'll find that the world is teeming with bandits out to rob you of your time. Your job is to avoid them, and the only way to do that is to know who they are. It doesn't matter if you've got the latest and greatest in technology, because these bandits can undermine even the best-laid time-saving plans.

Who are these bandits? You'll find them in offices throughout the world. So that you can know thine enemy, I'll list them here:

- Perfectionists

- People in love with the sound of their own voices

- People who love technology for the sake of technology

- Long-winded writers who find it hard to get to the point

- People who are impressed with their own authority

- People who are in over their heads

- People who aren't busy and don't have enough to do

- Egotists

- Bureaucrats

- Mind-changers

- Over-organizers

- People without goals

- Interrupters

- Decision avoiders

- People who put you on hold for longer than 30 seconds

- People who call you then put you on hold

- Compulsive changers

- Cars that spend a lot of time being repaired

- Technology that you don't understand

- Anyone in the world who does not cherish the value of time

The way to deal with these bandits is to be aware of them and how they erode your time. If you can identify them, you can eliminate them or, at least, your contact with them.

Along with the above bandits, there are time-wasting misguided efforts you may be guilty of yourself. Guerrillas are innocent of these charges:

- Reading unnecessary material

- Doing instead of delegating

- Daydreaming

- Worrying

- Rewarding themselves before they deserve the reward

- Being overly social at work

- Getting too involved in details that can handle themselves

- Skipping out or taking overly long lunches and breaks

- Being a slave to the telephone

- Being unable to say no to time bandits

- Not being focused on the task at hand

- Thinking that all time is created equal

- Not realizing they're wasting time

In his wonderful *What Color Is Your Parachute?*, Richard Nelson Bolles says, "I think almost everybody today has some problem with time. They are never, ever going to get done all that they want to do and therefore they have to establish priorities. They have to get a vision in their head of what is the most important to address." To do this, simply decide what tasks most merit your time right now, and then do those things. If you do this, you'll save time, save money, and eliminate stress, which author Bolles refers to as "the pain of time."

Tips for time-saving with technology

Technology by itself won't save time for you. But using that technology properly will do it. Ten tricks of the time-saving trade can allow technology to work its magic:

1. Rearrange your computer files to conform with the system you've created for your paperwork.

2. Keep copies of everything on clearly labeled backup disks. And don't feel that you have to print and store everything. You don't.

3. Open your mind to investing in a personal information manager program. There are many from which you may select and all of them can save you loads of time. Consider networking hardware that enables you to share not only peripherals but also information and resources. This can save you both time and money while increasing your productivity.

4. Invest in a high-speed modem, an ISDN (integrated services digital network) phone line, or a satellite modem if you do lots of downloading online. And be certain to set up your software to capitalize on that increased speed.

5. Update your contact manager and keep it current. Keep a printout near your phone so that you can change the information by hand when someone moves.

6. Invest in a cordless, hands-free phone so you can do routine chores while you're talking and listening.

7. Customize your software so that you can perform frequent functions at the touch of a button.

8. Function not only by your mouse but also by key commands. It may be tempting to use the mouse, but resisting that temptation will save time.

9. Set up style sheets if you consistently use the same styles in your newsletter, brochures, flyers, or letters—also if you use similar styles among these different documents. You don't want to be reformatting every time you create something new. You can do it once and be done with it.

10. If you can't invoice your customers with your current software, invest in a program that will do this for you. Many allow you to invoice, adjust inventory, update customer history, and keep track of total sales to date.

 ## Tips for time-saving without technology

Easy-tech—powerful and fast computers along with new simple-to-use software—can free up scads of time for you. But so can common sense. You don't have to be a rocket scientist or a computer maven to practice these tips:

1. Become adroit at saying "no."

2. If you're right-handed, place your phone on your left side and a pad and pen on your right side.

3. Set phone appointments with callers. This will help you avoid playing phone tag. When leaving messages, make them complete so that a return call is not necessary. Ask your callers to do the same. Interactivity is not a must on the telephone.

4. Realize that the downside of the Information Age is too much information, so use a data filter—which can be a computer program or a person—to highlight the information you should have, sparing you the time of finding it for yourself.

5. Make your phone calls before lunch and before quitting time so that people are already inclined to keep the conversation short. Many experts recommend making many of your calls during the last working hour on a Friday.

6. Group your phone calls. Make a flurry of them, then block out uninterrupted time for work.

7. Respond to business letters promptly and briefly. Encourage e-mail whenever you can.

8. Create customizable form letters so that you can respond to inquiries, solicitations, and invitations quickly and personally. Do the same for the thank-you notes you send and for those all-important follow-up letters.

9. Hire a part-time assistant. Scour your local college career center to find candidates. More and more small businesses—and college students—are discovering the joys of internships. It's one of the best of all win-win situations.

10. Ask for the first appointment of the day because it's the one least likely to start late and toss your entire day into disarray.

11. Group your appointments so that you can handle all of them in one day or one afternoon. Travel time is often wasted time. If you must travel, arrange to meet in other people's offices, because it's a whole lot easier to excuse yourself than to kick somebody out of your office.

12. Carry paperwork with you, or better yet, carry a laptop computer. This way, you can turn waiting time into productivity time. When in your car, use your car phone, listen to instructional tapes, and dictate memos—but please, keep your eyes on the road and your mind on driving safely. The accident rate is four times higher for car phone users.

A Technological Stitch in Time

A custom embroidery company in rural northern Idaho was outfitted with powerful, automated production equipment, but its business processes were still maintained by hand. Launched out of the owners' basement, the company now operates from a plant that regularly turns out 20,000 pieces a day: caps, T-shirts, jackets, and other garments emblazoned with logos and designs that are digitized and programmed into the embroidery machines.

With work orders for up to 15 customers being processed simultaneously, losing control at any stage could be disastrous, espe-cially given the thin operating margins. The firm implemented a program for systems and inventory management that could track an order from the start of the purchase order through production, shipping, and receiving. Having all of this information stored electronically not only improves the accuracy with which projects are managed and orders fulfilled, but it allows management to calculate machinery utilization and efficiency rates, resulting in more productive allocation of physical resources. Using technology to gain control over its business processes lets the company focus on delivering the high-quality service its customers have come to expect.

13. If you're self-employed, capitalize on the freedom granted you by self-employment and do your shopping and banking during off-peak hours. Guerrillas are not affected by the lunch-hour crush because they lunch before or after normal lunch hours.

 ## Do guerrillas watch the clock?

Guerrillas are never compulsive clock-watchers, because those people consider time an enemy. Instead, time, well-managed, can be your ally. So can people who are as aware of time as you are. Those are the people guerrillas connect with, hire, and train. If you're an expert on saving your time and you're surrounded by people oblivious to this fact, you'll be in for a lot of frustration. If you don't control your own time, you're probably working according to other people's priorities instead of your own.

The people who seem to make the worst use of their time are the ones who complain that there's never enough time. The truth is there is enough time if you know what to do with it. Benjamin Franklin must have agreed, because he said, "If we take care of the minutes, the years will take care of themselves."

Time is not money. But the way you use it and spend it can mean money. Says famed business consultant Peter Drucker, "Time is the scarcest resource, and unless it is managed, nothing else can be managed."

chapter **7**

The Benefits of Collaboration

The name of the game these days is collaboration—interdependence—more than independence, cooperation more than competition. Instead of thinking of yourself as an isolated business in an isolated office, think of yourself as part of a team. Instead of scanning the business horizon to spot whom you might be able to obliterate, tune your radar to businesses with which you might be able to cooperate. Instead of keeping all your assets to yourself—your information, your databases, your files, your computer programs, your Internet access, your equipment, your personnel, and your ideas—consider sharing them with others.

Share information and resources with your employees as well, with your suppliers, and with your customers. It used to be that information was something carefully guarded and never shared. But that has changed. The more you share information, the more valuable it becomes.

Light everybody's candle

Picture yourself with a lit candle in a dark room with 20 other people, each of whom is holding an unlit candle. If you use your candle to help light the other 20 candles, the room will no longer be dark, yet the brightness of your own candle will not be diminished. It's the same way with information. Keep it to yourself and it may help you a little. But if you share it, the information can help you a lot more while brightening the world for others.

In the past, information was valuable, so it was protected. In the present and future, it is valuable and so it is shared. That is a hallmark of the Information Age.

Guerrillas realize that they're living in a wired world and that the more they're connected, the more effectively they can run their businesses. They set up a communications infrastructure that enables them to communicate as they grow. That means they wire their offices for high speed ISDN (integrated services digital network) lines, for e-mail, and for networking with anyone who can benefit from it. They know in their hearts that if they don't embrace technology, they're operating with a competitive disadvantage.

Networking is sharing

"Network" to guerrillas means a lot more than ABC, CBS, or NBC. It represents an opportunity to share and, by doing so, to cut costs, increase productivity, improve customer service, reduce paperwork, save time, be more efficient, eliminate many meetings, and gain crucial flexibility.

The networks that guerrillas set up may start out small, with only a few computers connected to them, but they're expandable so they can grow as the business grows. No one realizes more than a guerrilla that an investment in technology is an investment that can pay rich dividends over time, and not a very long time.

It doesn't take long for guerrillas to discover the ease and low cost of networking, and that it's like being in the same office with people who may be a few miles or a few thousand miles away. Guerrillas give their employees remote access to files so that work can be accomplished at home, on the road, or right in a customer's office. And they're dazzled by the time-saving benefits of having several people work on a document or a project at the same time. What used to take five days because five people had to work on an assignment sequentially now takes one day because all five people can do their work at the same time.

 ## Who is networking now?

Of the estimated 7.1 million small businesses in the United States, 75 percent have PCs and 22 percent do computer networking. Those that network report a 20 percent increase in revenue per employee. And they say that the payback on their investment in networking took less than one year.

Research by Charles River Strategies is equally glowing. It reports that small companies with networks averaged at least 30 percent higher revenue per employee than those with no computers, and at least 11 percent higher than those with computers but no networks.

Networks installed by small businesses have five things in common:

1. They grant access to information to many or all of the key employees who are connected.

2. They allow businesses to render faster and more convenient customer service because many customers are now online.

3. They use network cables to transfer data.

4. They use network interface cards to connect devices, such as computers and printers, to the network cables.

5. They use a network operating system to control the flow of information over the network.

To network or not to network?

3Com, the largest networking company in the world, has developed a test to help you ascertain your readiness for networking. It's worth two minutes of your time to take it now:

- Do more than three employees share one printer?

- Do more than three employees share one fax machine?

- Do you plan to purchase another printer during the coming year?

- Do you plan to purchase another fax machine during the coming year?

- Do employees frequently share word processing documents and spreadsheets?

- Would employee productivity increase by implementing an automated accounting system that was available to more than one employee?

- Would employee productivity increase by having employees work from the same set of data such as a customer list or inventory database?

- Do more than two employees need Internet or e-mail access?

- Do any employees who currently use a computer at work telecommute or travel for business?

If you answered yes to none or to one of the questions, you probably don't need a network yet. If you answered yes to two or three questions, a network can add to the productivity and efficiency of your business. If you answered yes to four or more questions, a network can significantly increase your productivity and efficiency.

 ## Two kinds of networks

The easiest to install and least expensive network to get up and running is called a peer-to-peer network. It's decentralized

Sinking His Teeth into Technology

After 20 years of practicing, a New Orleans–based pediatric dentist was looking for a system that would bring administrative and communication processes up to the level of the state-of-the-art medical technologies he was already employing in his practice. Traditional manual processes were slowing his and his staff's abilities to generate, store, share, and access information within the office and with remote locations, such as hospitals and insurance offices. A computer consulting firm installed a new system in the dentist's office and had it running within two days, greatly enhancing the ways in which the dentist provides care to his patients.

Within the office, vital information is recorded and transmitted instantaneously. While he is providing real-time reports of treatment underway, up-to-the-minute information can be entered into a patient's chart by the dental assistant and viewed by parents in the waiting area. These processes have streamlined intraoffice communication, reduced the anxiety of patients and their parents, and ultimately have resulted in a 20–25 percent increase in patient flow. Meanwhile, all insurance claims are filed electronically: parents don't need to sign any forms; the support staff can submit claims efficiently in batches throughout the day; and claims are processed more quickly.

Electronic storage of records and information naturally improves patient care at a direct level as well. With the confidence that patient files and accounts are current, and with access to X-rays and video images at his fingertips—even at home—the doctor is able to respond immediately to emergencies, and consult electronically with colleagues if necessary, thereby increasing the speed with which diagnoses can be made and appropriate care provided.

and ideally suited to small offices with five or fewer computers to connect. No computer is in control; each computer workstation is equal.

Picture it as a small group of computers connected by a string—the cable—that allows each one to share files with the others. Users can also e-mail, share spreadsheets and word processing programs, and share fax machines and modems.

Figure on a cost of around $3,000 to connect five computers. That will cover software and an easily installed network interface card.

The alternative to a peer-to-peer network, called a client/server network, runs from $5,000 to $10,000 and enables you to share larger items such as databases. It connects six or more computers, one of which is the central computer, called the server. The server stores all the programs and files for everyone else in the network, each of whom is a client.

This kind of network provides remote access—the ability for employees who travel or telecommute to access networked applications and printers from anywhere on earth using only a telephone line and a modem. It also enables office employees to access Internet service providers with a shared modem rather than requiring one modem for each user, a substantial savings. It provides more speed and better performance than a peer-to-peer network.

 ## What kind of network is right for you?

Once peer-to-peer networks discover the heady benefits of speedy communications and the economies of sharing, they don't wait long to become client/server networks. If you have six or more computers right now, or anticipate having that many, open your mind to investing in a client/server network. It's just the ticket if you want your employees or coworkers to be able to connect to your network while they're traveling. If you have at least three employees who could contribute to your company's effectiveness by going online and accessing the Net or sending e-mail outside your company, you should investigate a client/server network before your competitors do. Your guiding light: Never forget that the prime beneficiaries of your sojourn into networking should be your profitability and your customers.

The cost of a network is really based upon many factors: the size of your business; equipment you may already own; the type of network that will work best for you; and the software you'll need. An average small business network for six employees runs $9,800, assuming you already have six work-stations and two printers. That figure includes the $1,500 allocated for installation and training. The initial investment you make will soon be paid back to you in increased profits. Everything after that is gravy.

The lone wolf is gone

So what's happened to the age of the lone wolf entrepreneur? It's going the way of the Bronze Age, as technology enables the world to work in a brand new way, collaborating and connecting faster and farther than ever, yet easier and more affordably than ever. Small businesses now have the ability to communicate as fast as the giants, to grant coworkers instant access to one another, and to perform far better customer service than before networking came into its prime. Networking allows small businesses to respond more rapidly to change, which is one of the benefits of being a small business in the first place.

The whole idea of computer networking started back in the early eighties, and it's been growing ever since. Costs have been dropping, speed increasing, and technology getting simpler to use all along. 3Com reports sales increases of 40 percent for each of the three years starting in 1994. The Gallup Organization says that small business will increase spending on computer networks by 280 percent in 1997 over 1996. When asked, "How essential a part of your business has the network become?", over 96 percent of small businesses surveyed by Charles River Strategies said "somewhat" or "very essential." The lone wolf is now part of a pack.

Three examples of networks in action

Consider the ten-person insurance office that had six PCs, one laser printer, and three ink-jet printers. Before networking, if an employee needed to print a final copy, he or she would have to carry a diskette to the computer connected to the laser printer. With networking, the employee can laser-print documents without leaving his or her desk. That's a saving in time and money, since funds that used to be spent on individual desktop printers can now be used for a single high-quality printer that can be shared by all employees.

A small accounting firm was run by a person who had Internet access to the latest IRS regulations. But his employees didn't. Purchasing a modem and phone line for each employee would have been pricey. So the boss installed a network with a shared high-speed modem, giving all of his staff access to the Internet through a single ISDN line, which is also used for phone calls and sending faxes. The result? A saving of money and time along with instant responsiveness to customer needs.

A twelve-person public relations agency assigned the responsibility for coordinating the review of documents to several employees. Before networking, these employees printed the documents then handed them to their associates for review. After networking, drafts were distributed electronically. Reviewers could make comments directly on the electronic copy then return documents to the writer. This saved money by significantly reducing paperwork and saved time by shortening the time-consuming review cycle.

How most small businesses use networking

More than 75 percent of small businesses use their networks for print sharing, according to IDC Research, making this the single most common application of network technology. The next most common network application is sharing files and common databases, such as scheduling, accounting, and sales prospecting. This clearly indicates that networks are actually changing the way small companies do business.

One of the fastest growing network applications is accounting software, with 70 percent of small businesses using accounting packages. Payroll, inventory management, and tax preparation have also enjoyed healthy increases in popularity among small businesses that have embraced the benefits of networking.

 ## Talking dollars and cents

It isn't very easy to accurately project the impact that a network will have on your small business, but here are some guidelines to help you:

- You can calculate how much faster specific functions can be performed with a network, then multiply the minutes saved by the employees' salaries. If you figure on saving three minutes by printing a document on a network rather than carrying it to a printer and waiting for it to print, and if you pay an average salary of $20 per hour, you save $1 each time an employee uses the network to print. If 10 of your 20 employees print three documents a day, the network will save you $30 a day, or $7,500 a year—just on printing.

- You can share printers, fax machines, and modems if you have a network. By installing one, you save the $1,200 cost of an additional laser printer or plain paper fax machine. You also save time because employees can use printers and fax machines without ever leaving their desks.

- Your customer service reps can take orders at least twice as quickly using a centrally located database as they can the old-fashioned manual way, which also eliminates your need to hire more reps as your business grows. The idea is to have growth equate with prosperity rather than increased expenses.

Whom do you network with?

That's the right question, and here's the right answer: You network with anyone who can empower your business while becoming more empowered themselves. I don't love using such a New Age word as empower, but it's the right word to describe what computers do for small business. Connecting to a network should always be a win-win-win situation, with you winning, your fellow networker winning, and your customer winning because of your collaboration.

That means you'll probably connect with some or all of your coworkers or employees, that your network may include some or all of your customers, and that it might also hook up with people who provide services for you. Guerrillas are always on the lookout for fusion marketing partners, other businesses that share your prospects and high standards. When you see a TV commercial for a soft drink that suddenly becomes a fast food spot and ends up plugging the latest Disney movie, you're seeing fusion marketing as it's practiced by big-time guerrillas.

But most fusion marketing occurs on a much smaller scale with companies connecting for the mutual benefit of their customers, sharing the costs of marketing while increasing their exposure. The Internet has given rise to more fusion marketing than ever, as businesses of all sizes link with the common goal of improving customer service and communication. One thing all of these companies have in common is an awareness of the need for allies.

External networking doesn't have to be limited to fusion marketing. You can share information and resources with suppliers, vendors—even competitors. Technology facilitates new kinds of relationships, and can redefine corporate boundaries.

A small business can become an information hub for a geographically dispersed community. One recreation company in, say, Moab, Utah, can serve as the tourist guide to every other tourist-oriented business in that area of the state. It can network with the other companies for the benefit of all companies, and especially for the good of the tourist.

An advertising agency can link with an interactive agency, a direct marketing agency, a web site developer, a media-buying service, a music composer, a TV director, a photographer, an artist, a research firm, and a whole lot more. I think I've made my point. Now you've got to make your network.

Networking comes in every size and shape, limited only by your imagination. To do it properly, don't think of yourself but of your customer. What allied products and services might you link with to make that customer happier? I'll bet you can come up with a long list.

 ## What every business needs

Every business needs allies. No matter what business you're in, you should be able to find allies in related businesses online, and joining forces can increase marketing presence for all of you. For example, you and another web site operator can agree to exchange links or to feature one another's information on your sites. Or you can plan joint promotions or contests with several businesses, with each business contributing time, money, or merchandise in exchange for a sponsorship notice. Think about other businesses that are seeking the same customers you seek, then contact those businesses about how you can work together to boost your online marketing punch. If you're an attorney, might you link up with a CPA? Of course. And vice versa.

 ## Stop being so technical

Although guerrilla businesses enjoy the abundant benefits of computer networking and continue to discover even more advantages to being in ten places at once, they never neglect the more high-touch form of personal networking. They attend gatherings of their peers and distinguish themselves by the number of questions they ask, speaking rarely of themselves and frequently of those they're meeting.

Their antennae are attuned to collaborative opportunities. They gauge their success at the networking function not by how many business cards they hand out, but by how many potential fusion business opportunities they spot. They are in a permanent quest to enlarge their network. They're well aware that there's a movement afoot called "collaborative entrepreneurship," and they know that means networks. Small businesses are working with other small businesses, with large companies, with buyers, sellers, and a wide assortment of allied businesses, to share talent, technology, and capital, not to mention information.

Potential members of your high-touch network include: competitors far away from you, competitors who are nearby, fellow entrepreneurs in or out of your community, investors, lenders, landlords, and online businesses.

What you can share

You can share hardware and software with members of your high-tech network. You can share databases and files. With members of your high-touch network, you can share plans, technology, management skills, customer service, workspace, purchasing power, marketing, and information.

These alliances should be entered into with the idea that they are temporary rather than permanent. Their only purposes should be mutual profits and increased customer satisfaction. If an arrangement works out for a single project or for one year, it can be extended. Perhaps some businesses with which you ally yourself will later hook up to your high-tech network. Possibly you'll connect to theirs.

Thinking collaboration

The important thing is for you to think in terms of collaborating rather than going it alone. Whether you collaborate with employees or other businesses, you'll quickly see why being a

Blueprint for Growth

An architecture firm with 25 employees in New York and two employees in a satellite Los Angeles office was bursting at the seams, concerned that it could not keep up with its growing client list or efficiently manage the vast amounts of information that needed to be shared in the development and launch of a project. Already using sophisticated computer-aided design programs to render drawings, the firm decided to hire a computer consultant to help incorporate technology into more aspects of its operations.

At one level, the new technology has increased the efficiency and speed of communications. E-mail and word processing capabilities allow the staff to keep a running record of ideas, feedback, and decisions, especially important when the team kicks into high-production mode. An electronic notebook makes everyone's schedules transparent. Dial-in remote networking lets the two partners, who often travel, gain access to all files in the office. The company's web page serves as a digital portfolio, showcasing its projects to visitors worldwide.

But at a more fundamental level, the technology has changed the way the firm works. For example, there are no secretaries; all clerical and administrative tasks can be handled by the architects themselves. The collaborative potential is enormous: instead of individuals working on separate drawings, six or seven people can work together simultaneously, increasing both creativity and productivity in the process. At the other end of the spectrum, a single person can "multitask," performing several functions at the same time, from conducting Internet research to tinkering with a drawing to sending correspondence. According to one of the partners, the most significant effect has been the ability to grow the types of projects they can handle without significantly increasing staff.

rugged individualist is no longer where it's at, and why collaborative efforts are increasingly recognized as the foundation for entrepreneurial success.

Connecting with others has never been as inexpensive, as simple, and as well-advised as it is today. It has existed for a long time: when Thomas Edison talked about his new filaments with the Corning Glass Company the lightbulb was born; that was pure collaboration and cooperation. But the concept has taken a quantum leap during the past decade, and that was just for openers.

 ## Computers, the Internet, and networking

Remember when you first started reading about personal computers, then a little while later the media began running stories about them every day and all over the place? Remember when the exact same thing happened with the Internet? Well, the same thing is happening again with networking. It is rapidly becoming identified in both its high-tech and high-touch forms as the hallmark of our interdependent future. With networking, a small business in reality can act like a big business in practice, collaborating with others all over the world to the delight of its customers and accountants.

Collaboration, cooperation, partnering, co-marketing, fusion, tying in, jointly promoting—the idea of teaming up with others has many names. But the spirit was summed up by the Beatles when they sang, "With a Little Help from My Friends." Collaboration is happening today, and if you're not letting it happen in your business, you're not listening to the music.

chapter **8**

▓ Mining the Treasures of the Internet

Guerrillas know that the rainbow leading to the pot of gold passes through cyberspace. They realize that the Internet is not only an information superhighway but also a communication, commercial, and recreation superhighway. It's a new medium of marketing, easily the most comprehensive ever devised, beneficial to buyer and seller.

Almost daily, the Internet is gaining acceptance, clarity, and accessibility, making it a boon for online commerce for those who enter that superhighway knowing the rules of the road. Once there weren't any rules, but now new ones are being created, and guerrillas are using them as guideposts to profitability.

Guerrillas know there is a major difference between using the Internet, which is quite easy to do, and abusing the Internet, which is even easier to do. For proof of the latter, just check the junk mail in your e-mailbox, or surf the web to see how many web sites are speaking to nobody in particular.

 One weapon among many

The single biggest key to success on the Internet is to understand marketing and how the Internet fits into marketing. The

Internet is only one marketing weapon and must be combined with other weapons to be a winner. The guerrilla at the controls must see how the Net fits into the whole marketing picture, then launch a full-scale marketing program. The Internet may be the biggest breakthrough in the history of marketing, but it is not marketing itself.

If you intend to use the Internet to market your offerings—as I advise you to do and predict you will—I hope you see it in the context of your prospects' lives. You would never walk into a party and say, "Okay everybody, take your minds off of yourselves and concentrate only on me because I'm the only one who matters. If you don't like what I say, you can just leave." Sounds boorish! But that's what most web sites seem to say. They offer only the site owner's perspective. Guerrillas see things from their visitors' perspectives, recognizing that almost all visitors love to learn and that the Internet provides an exceptional opportunity to give them stuff to learn.

What I do for a living

One morning I woke up and realized that I had switched careers without even noticing it. When I went to sleep, I was a writer and speaker. But when I awoke and read the daily newspaper, it occurred to me that in the current era I really am a content provider. I provide content in the form of talks, seminars, books, columns, articles, and online chat sessions and web pieces. And it dawned on me that being a content provider in an age when information is currency is a good thing.

I'm still in awe of how the Net makes for a more efficient world. I've mined its treasures for only four years, so I'm still discovering on a regular basis the wonders it holds for me and my family. It is with great restraint that I limit this chapter to discussing the use of the Internet to beautify your bank account. When I see my wife spend untold hours online viewing art from the Louvre, I know the full potential of the Net has little to do with anybody's bank account.

What you do for a living

If you're counting on a web site to contribute to your revenue and you don't see yourself as a content provider, you should rethink your definition of yourself. No matter how you market online, underneath it all you are providing content. The more that content can be of benefit to your prospects, the better you'll thrive online. Guerrillas who wish to market on the Internet realize that web sites are only one of the myriad of marketing weapons the Net makes available to them. Among the others are storefronts, newsgroups, chat rooms, e-mail, classified sections, search engines, and directories.

 ## The new way of the new world

There are two relatively new words that keep popping up all over the place: Internet and web. The Internet is a series of connected computer networks located throughout the world. The World Wide Web is a system of Internet servers that supports specially formatted documents; it's just one part of the Internet.

The world is learning to buy things in a new way—by going to web sites. I buy a new car every 25 years like clockwork and decided to buy my most recent car using only the web, just to see if it really could be done. I accessed many web sites and read the brochures. I checked the recommendations of magazines such as *Car and Driver, Road and Track,* and *Consumer Reports.* After picking the make and model that sounded best, I did my price shopping online.

Amazingly, everything worked. The experience was pleasant. I was never put under pressure. The car was great. The price was dynamite. The process took a fraction of the time that old-fashioned car shopping would. And I made a very informed decision. I know that it took 40 years for the zipper to go from being invented and patented to being understood and used. I don't think it will take that long for online commerce to hit its peak.

Getting better all the time

I think the Internet has been under-hyped, if anything. The best is yet to come, for the Internet is still in its infancy. It continues to improve almost daily, adding substance and style, simplicity and speed.

In some parts of the world, subscriptions to online services are growing at the rate of 20 percent per month. Dr. Louis Patler of The Bit Group also reports that in 1996, for the first time ever, PC sales were higher than TV sales, and there was more e-mail—177 billion pieces—than snail mail—a piddling 157 billion pieces. Perhaps most startling of all, there are now more computer literate first-graders in the world than computer literate first-grade teachers. Those first-graders are growing up in a neighborhood that includes the Internet. They are very comfortable in its environment, and comfort is one of the first things you should seek as well.

The companies that will fare best on the Internet during the coming century are those gaining the most intimacy with it during the present century.

 What guerrillas know

Guerrillas know that without any training at all they can create and post their own web sites. Remarkably easy-to-use software makes this possible. Even small and start-up guerrillas can afford it. Their sites can wow every surfer in sight and open the door to the cybervault. The combination of a powerful offer of a truly desirable benefit, the credibility that comes with a professional online presentation, and speedy response time will open that vault.

Guerrillas remember that time is far more important than money, and that even as the speed of data transmission gets faster each year, time continues to grow in value. They know that online visitors don't want you to waste their time. Their sites don't overuse glitz and techno-gimmicks to attract viewers. They don't squander their guests' time by forcing them to download unnecessary images.

Content rules

The key to the online kingdom is content. Juicy, exclusive, valuable content will bring in the viewers the first time, then bring them back for more of the same. Guerrilla content is heavy with text and laden with subheads for easy digestion while reading or scrolling, on a screen or a piece of paper.

A guerrilla's web site provides information the competitors' web sites aren't providing, both in quality and quantity. It changes regularly. It is fresh and new, appealing not to the world in general but to your target prospects specifically. It demonstrates a noble purpose of marketing by offering those prospects data that can help them succeed, whether at making money, attracting a mate, enjoying a holiday, or losing weight. People using the Internet aren't really as interested in you as they are in learning. Content teaches, and that's why it reigns supreme in online marketing.

 ## A session and not a thing

Using the Internet without abusing it is viewing your web site not as a thing but as a session. That means every session should be different from every other session, yet each one must be directed right at your target audience, providing them with information that can propel them to their own goals. The more interactivity your site offers, the better.

Make e-mailing ultra-easy. Ask questions. Allow space for answers. Solicit comments. Hold polls. Ask for opinions. Request advice. Put the ball in your prospect's court. From the very start, get used to seeing your web site not through your own eyes but through those of a prospect.

Make certain that your web site content connects closely with the specific purpose of your marketing and your marketing theme. Your site is both the voice of your company and a conduit for individual service. Think of it as the display windows to your department store. Put exciting new things there continuously to motivate shoppers to come back.

Out of control in cyberspace

Maybe you can slide down a snow-covered mountain on any two pieces of wood, but you'll do it with far more control on equipment designed especially to get you down that mountain

DEAR JAY,

I am a novice in marketing via the Internet and have noticed the incredible growth in web sites hawking all kinds of multilevel marketing programs and business opportunities. I decided to try one of those programs that offer your own "Free Web Page," because it sounded neato and high-tech and potentially lucrative. The problem is that when you register your page with web site search engines, so is every other marketer. What is the best way to distinguish yourself from the others on the bandwagon? (When I do a search for my web site, it is usually way, way down the list.)

One method, of course, is direct marketing via e-mail, listing the specific address of the web site. The only hits I get are through this method. But I was expecting (or at least hoping) to get some hits from listing the opportunity with the search engines. The one thing I have learned is that marketing over the Internet is not automatic. You still must dig up the customers. — MGD

DEAR MGD,

Well, I'm glad you've learned that marketing on the Net isn't automatic. If you don't know marketing, the Internet can't shine for you. You've got to have as many links as possible, market your site like a guerrilla, and view the Net as a marketing medium and not a miracle worker. As far as distinguishing yourself in search engines goes, remember that people go to

safely and effectively. No matter how computer savvy you may be, you don't want to be out of control in the new world of the Internet. Web page development software has been designed especially to get you online safely and effectively. It prevents you from overlooking important details about such things as

search engines to search for something specific, so, to a degree, they need to be looking for a topic related to you to begin with. But here are some recommendations I have to help your site stand out.

On your web site, invite readers to make your site a favorite by adding it to their list of favorites or book-marked sites. Get it listed all over the place by submit-ting web site information to the following sites, each of which will happily list your site free in numerous search engines and directories: www.submit-it.com, www.netcreations.com/postmaster, and www.mgroup.com. You can also pay a nominal charge and get it listed in over 100 directory and search engines by contacting AAA Internet Promotions at www.websitepromote.com/home.htm.

I also recommend surfing the Internet to determine who your competitors are, what you do better or differ-ently than they do, and what competitive advantages you should focus upon in marketing yourself. Feature these advantages on your web site and in all of your marketing.

Finally—and this is just an electronic approach to a standard tool in the guerrilla's arsenal—use smart PR. Try sending a well-crafted "media alert" via e-mail to all the online sites that promote other sites. If they like your web site, maybe they'll highlight it and offer a direct link. Just ask. It costs you almost nothing to do this, and the result may triple your hits! — Jay

registration with search vehicles, while giving wings to your creativity and providing you with momentum and confidence in cyberspace.

If you really want to perform your own brain surgery, feel free to experiment. But if you're going to market on the Internet, the hands-on, in-control, understanding-by-doing software of the day is mandatory armament.

 ## Launching is just the start

The day you launch your web site is Day One. From Day One on, you've got to make your site better and publicize it online and offline. Guerrillas actually plan the freshening of their sites when they plan their launch. Their goal is to make their sites increase in value consistently, and they know that content increases value.

Who better to entice to your site than a person who already knows where it is? So guerrillas make it easy for people to make return visits, and they encourage regular visits. To lure visitors back, guerrillas promise new things, then live up to those promises, even exceed them. For example, on my site I might promise ten new guerrilla marketing weapons to be unveiled and then unveil 20.

 ## Responding is the heart

When a prospect visits your web site, regardless of how good it looks, that prospect is not made to feel singled out or unique. But when he or she sends you an e-mail and you respond instantly, then the prospect feels special. He knows he's receiving individual service and feels on a deeper level that he'll be treated by you like an individual and not a member of a group.

Guerrillas know well that of the millions of people on the Internet, only a teeny-tiny number take the time and trouble to write. So the guerrillas always and instantly take the time and trouble to respond. If they're too busy, they designate someone else to do it.

Rapid and certain response may be the single most important factor in building a loyal customer base. Plan at the outset how you'll arrange for speedy communications to ensure that you'll succeed at marketing online

 ## Not linking is not thinking

The moment you launch your site you should be fine-tuning your radar for fusion marketing opportunities—connecting with others to spread the marketing word while sharing the marketing investment. Fusion marketing describes that phenomenon of joining a frequent flier program and learning that the airline has connected for marketing purposes with a hotel chain, a car rental firm, and probably a cruise line. There's a whole lot of fusing going on, especially on the level of small business and most especially on the Internet where everybody and their cousin can link together. Free links, traded links and small-fee links can make you marketing partners with businesses around the corner and around the world. Not linking is not thinking.

Your job in finding links is to locate businesses that share the same kind of prospects as you, the same kind of standards, and the same kind of enthusiasm about marketing. Each is a potential gateway to your site and gateways mean visitors. Surely you can support each other online, but you also might benefit from teaming up offline or with a computer network.

Alliances with the goal of profits for all are springing up all over the world, and no more fertile ground for them exists than online. I look up the web site for Grand Junction, Colorado, and see that the city has linked with many restaurants and bed and breakfast establishments in the area. Makes me happy to get that information. Makes the business owners happy to get my business. They're one big happy cyberfamily and they're willing to let anyone in on their family secrets.

Going online? Think offline.

The moment you go online is the moment you should begin thinking of how to promote that site offline. Far more people reside offline than online—including onliners—so you've got to build awareness of your site in the mass media of radio, TV, newspapers, and magazines, as well as in direct mailings, with signs, and in directories.

Add your web site address to your business cards, letterhead, brochures, flyers—anywhere that you'd list your phone number or address. Affix it to envelopes, invoices, catalogs, postcards, Yellow Pages ads, press releases, and newsletters. More than one company has created a radio and TV jingle using its web site address as the words. Even if you rarely advertise, you'll be able to generate awareness of your web site with traditional ads.

DEAR JAY,

I am currently launching a small golf apparel business on the web. I understand the marketing aspects of this and what it takes to be successful at any business. The question is: How do I know what links to make? Should they be in areas related to my product? Or should the links be in totally unrelated product categories? The next question is: How would you assess the number of sales? Should it be like direct mail or mail orders, where a 3 percent return is considered great?
— Steve

DEAR STEVE,

It's always a pleasure receiving e-mail from golfers about links. Make your links to any groups that are even vaguely connected to your business. Since your business happens to be golf apparel, that means firms involved in golf, travel, lodging, tennis, fashion, and probably even more, such as country clubs. And don't

What proud new parents do

Announce your new creation to the world. It's a web site! Just as you'd notify potential and current clients of a change of address, you ought to announce your new web page with a special mailer. Send formal announcements to your customer base and your referral sources. Send postcard mailers to your prospects. It's a new world that you live in online, and you want to share your place in it with others.

You can reach many top-drawer prospects in schools, clubs, businesses, and throughout your community. Making presentations to these groups provides guerrillas with cost-free, fertile forums for disseminating web site addresses as well as for establishing authority and credibility.

Specialized newsgroups and forums can provide a ready-made audience for your products and services. As you con-

---

forget the media addressing those industries, such as the golf channel and the many golfing publications. Select links to companies that have the same kinds of prospects and standards as you. But make sure the links are related. For instance, you might assume that http://www.pga.com would be a great link from your golf apparel web page. But it may actually belong to the Pea Growers Association of Alabama. That URL does actually belong to the Professional Golfers' Association, but you get the idea. Unrelated links on your web page may confuse some potential customers and forfeit some of your credibility. So think before you link.

As for estimating sales, I can't do that yet. But precision measuring technology will soon enable sales to be accurately predicted based upon hits, click-throughs, time spent, and other criteria. Still, that's the right question to ask, and the first to answer will win the game.
— Jay

verse with these people in one-on-one situations, in chats or via e-mail, attach a four-line Internet signature after your name, including your web site address, e-mail address, phone number, and fax number.

Your offline world teems with people who would love to know where to find you online. To what groups do they belong? What newspapers do they read? To which magazines do they subscribe? What trade shows do they attend? What do they have in common? Your answers to these questions will lead you to the right offline media in which to promote your web site.

 ## Bad PR and how to get it

An easy way to make a lot of enemies in a hurry is to announce a web site that is not entirely up and running or that has nearly as many bugs as the Amazon rain forest. To avoid such a situation, do a mailing to your best friends and associates announcing your site. Encourage them to order without risk so you can identify any problems with your site before the general public begins to visit it. Make your mistakes with your best friends because they'll understand. Forewarn them that they'll be guinea pigs.

Guerrilla retailers wouldn't dream of having a grand opening until their stores have been open at least a month so they can work out the kinks. The same should be true of your web site. Get it up to speed. Debug it. Then let the world know about it.

 ## Guerrilla marketing online basic training

- Know how to communicate. That means spelling correctly, punctuating properly, being concise, getting to the point, and using language skillfully.

Focused on the Web

A company providing high-quality professional stock photography images is using its web site to redefine the boundaries of its business. Within three years of its founding in 1991, the company had established an online presence, and by 1995 was a pioneer in promoting its products over the World Wide Web. Not satisfied with simply using the web as a storefront, the owners started to explore new ways to deliver content to and communicate with their customers. In an effort to promote the site as a product delivery channel, they had cataloged over 15,000 digitized images by 1996, with plans to increase that number to 100,000. The firm began to offer complimentary online starter packets, and makes sure that members of its customer service staff are web-savvy.

By 2000 they expect at least half of their business to be conducted electronically. Open 24 hours a day, the site is always being visited by at least three or four people, from locations as remote as Iceland and Malaysia. At heavier traffic hours 30–60 visitors may be at the site concurrently, downloading images and requesting information.

By recognizing how technology could facilitate the actual delivery of its products, the firm has made its web site far more than a purveyor of information and an order fulfillment vehicle.

■ Get to know the territory. The terrain is unfamiliar in cyberspace, so learn how to get comfortable in forums, newsgroups, conferences, chat sessions, classified ad sections, web sites, and electronic publications. Learn how to post messages to forums and newsgroups, how to reply to somebody else's message, how to upload to a forum library. Know how to handle e-mail: sending, reading, replying, forwarding, printing, and saving it. These activities should be second nature to you before you launch so that you don't have to think about them in the heat of battle.

■ Be aggressive. You are invisible in the online world and you'll remain that way until you start participating. Your job is to participate in discussion groups,

Dear Jay,

We have been in the computer business now for just over one year and have noticed the new methods of reaching our customers and prospects. Six months ago Internet access was still a luxury, with pricing ranging from $80/40 hours to $150/unlimited in our area. Due to these inflated prices, we relied on some of the older technologies, such as the BBS (bulletin board system). With the BBS, we could provide our prospects and customers with online documentation, software utilities, and information on upcoming events. The use of a BBS also provided us a method of keeping up with who had logged on, providing information that permitted us to bring in the prospect or to keep in touch after the sale.

Our question deals with your advice on establishing a web page on the Internet. We are a small business located in a small college town. Would a web page be beneficial to us or any other business located in a remote region? Or would you recommend the use of another service such as the BBS? In addition, wouldn't a web page create possible problems of too many responses to handle, along with the impersonal aspect?
— WD

Dear WD:

It sounds to me as though you've been doing a lot of smart things, especially your concentration on retaining current customers. Another smart thing you can do is to realize that a web site can augment everything else you are doing. Don't think of it as an alternative to a BBS, but as a supplement. Continue your activities with the BBS and provide even more data about yourself with your web site.

A BBS enables you to market with text only, so if you want people to see what you're offering, a web site might be better. In terms of trends, BBS marketing has been taking a back seat to the highly graphical nature of the World Wide Web. Browsing the web is also easier for your customers than accessing a BBS. Search engines enable them to find you without even knowing your URL. And a web site portrays your company as cutting edge. While you and others have continued to find some use for BBS marketing, some potential customers might consider this approach outdated—like a black-and-white TV set with rabbit ears, while a web site is like a five-foot-screen color TV with a satellite dish and theater sound.

A web site on the Internet gives you the opportunity to support your existing customers more than you could with a BBS. The advent of the Internet is also a boon to businesses in remote locations because it enables them to join a global community. The more time you spend surfing, the more you'll realize that. As far as growing too fast is concerned, you can control your speed of growth by being very selective. Although up to 50 million people use the Internet these days, you'll still find that it ends up being a very personal medium because you'll be dealing one-on-one with many of those people. Some will be right in your community and others may be across the world from you. Your relationships may start out online, but can then move to telephone and even face-to-face meetings. Even after you're mining the BBS market and attracting new customers with your web site, you'll still find that those are only two of the myriad weapons of marketing that you can use to abet your cause. The way you think about marketing up till now makes me believe that you'll make it work for you even better if you enlist as much aid as you can get, meaning a web site, BBS, e-mailing, and warm, instant follow-up to those prospects who fit your customer profile. — Jay

post announcements, publish articles of value, hold conferences, seek out listings in online directories, search for linking partners, get some action going on your web site. Your presence must be consistently maintained with new articles, fresh promotions, even real-time discussion sessions right at your site.

- Pay close attention. Visit your own site regularly and respond within 24 hours to all requests e-mailed to your site. Check the position of your classified ad to be sure it's still near the top of the message list where it's most likely to be read. Keep posting messages to forums and newsgroups and continue to check for replies to them. Order from yourself once in a while to make sure the machinery is well oiled.

- Personalize as much as you can. Even though guerrillas use automatic responding technology that allows their computers to send e-mail automatically to people who mention a specific word or phrase in their own e-mail, the powers of cyberspace smile upon those who personalize each message. Guerrillas do all in their power to establish warm, human bonds.

- Follow up with tenacity. In the darkness of cyberspace it's easy to get lost, and prospects forget you lightning-fast. Once guerrillas establish contact, they knock themselves out to maintain it. They do this with order confirmation, e-mailed thank-yous, bimonthly or quarterly e-mail follow-ups, brochures, catalogs, and anything else customers might find helpful. Being guerrillas, they care about ongoing relationships much more than quick one-time sales.

- Know what customers love to read about. They do not love to read about you. They do love to read about their dreams, their problems, the solutions you can provide to their problems, and the benefits you can bestow upon them—any information that is of value to them. They are spending more and more time on their computers and are growing more and more open to online commerce.

- Realize what makes online commerce so special. It's not the technology. It's not merely the speed and convenience. As with any kind of commerce, it's the strength of your offer. If it is extraordinary, online commerce will do wonders for you. If it is ordinary, all the technology in the world won't help. You still must find an appealing way to offer value while inspiring confidence. If marketing your offering would work offline, marketing it online can bring you success even faster. And if it sells in Keokuk, there's a good chance it will sell in Kuala Lumpur.

 ## The weekly surf

If you want the best education possible about the Internet, find it on a one-hour weekly surf through the Net. Look for anything and be prepared for everything. Find yourself and find your competitors. Check their web sites as closely as you check your own, and be certain to check your own.

Be on the alert for great ideas as well as terrible ideas, knowing you'll learn from both. This regular surfing session will keep you abreast of what's happening and what can happen, as well as keeping you one step ahead, which is exactly where your prospects hope you'll be. Guerrillas are inherently curious, but in cyberspace their exploring instinct is turned up even higher because they know their audience loves new things.

Willie Sutton said he robbed banks because that was where the money was. Guerrilla marketers go online because, more and more, that's where the customers are. Online guerrillas reach hundreds, thousands, or even tens of thousands of potential customers by spending a few hundred dollars a month or less. They are able to zero in on their customers and market to them in a brand new, much better way than they ever could before.

Many companies already say that the Internet contributes to their profitability. Many more businesses will make fortunes using the Internet in the year 2000 and beyond. I can tell you right now which ones they will be: They'll be the guerrillas who learned how to get the most from the Internet right now.

chapter 9

High-Tech/ High-Return Marketing

For ages, businesses have been in a quest for high-return marketing, but it is only during the present age that they've been able to tap into the awesome power of technology to succeed at their goal. By employing it, many business owners are enjoying a higher return than ever on their marketing investment. And that investment is lower than ever. Technology gets the credit. Technology and sanity.

There are new kinds of high-return marketing these days, such as rewarding customers and wooing prospects in luxury boxes at professional sporting events. And there's the remarkably high-return marketing that guerrillas employ when they speak for free at clubs, winning new customers with their expertise and warmth, not to mention their generosity with their time.

A vast and inviting array

But the array of technological methods small businesses can use to market is so vast and so inviting that I'm singling it out in this chapter. It's so new and economical that I'm hoping you'll consider all of the methods, then use as many as make sense for you.

I know at least ten ways that technology can boost your profitability. And I'm realizing that nine of these ways didn't exist as I was starting my marketing career, and that everyone was oblivious of the tenth—faxing. One of these ten methods of high-tech/high-return marketing by itself provides a juicy arsenal of 27 guerrilla marketing weapons that you can employ (see item number 6 on the list that appears later in this chapter). It's one thing to be able to employ one of these weapons. It's a different ball game altogether if you employ a multitude of these weapons.

But if you're a guerrilla you will.

 Guerrilla pondering

Technology now provides so many avenues for marketing a small business that merely pondering the options establishes momentum toward traveling to where they lead. If you realize that you can create gift certificates in your office, you might open your mind to offering them to your prospects and customers. If you discover the excitement and the instant rush of marketing in online conferences, you might add them to your existing marketing program.

Thanks to recent technology, you can employ high-powered marketing tactics and techniques that were way out of your reach a short time ago. They were too complex, too expensive, too filled with bugs. Well, the bugs are gone—not all of them, but nearly all. The prices have dropped dramatically. And technology is now an equal IQ opportunity. It's easier to use than ever, as the people who design the equipment and write the user manuals seem to have increased in intelligence. Either they have or the entire planet has, because you no longer need training to be a nerd.

Lots of the rules have been changed by easy-tech. You don't have to be an artist to be creative. You don't have to be a marketing genius to market with genius. You don't have to be near people to closely connect with people. You don't have to

The World Comes to Utah

A family-owned store specializing in Native American jewelry is using the Internet to make the world its marketplace. Established in St. George, Utah, in 1951, the store was originally conceived as a typical small-town jeweler and watch repair shop. Over time the proprietors recognized the demand for unique, locally-produced jewelry, and began to service gift shops and hotel chains.

As the Internet revolution began to take shape, the family realized that the online medium was perfectly suited for their products. Working with an Internet service provider, they established a web site to showcase their company and its hand-made products. The greatest benefit has been the company's ability to take its wholesale and retail businesses worldwide. Through the web site they have discovered a very strong demand for Native American jewelry in Japan; to meet the needs of their Japanese customers and distributors, they found a partner in California (via the Internet!) who has translated the entire catalog into Japanese and created Japanese order forms. Other business is being generated in Australia and Slovenia. The Internet has allowed this small-town jeweler to promote and sell its products around the world, identify and respond to new customer segments, and improve communication with its network of vendors and distributors.

have a publisher to be published. You don't have to be a big business to earn profits like one.

Technology gives small businesses the chance to market aggressively without spending aggressively, to profit lavishly without risking foolishly.

 # Where guerrilla technology begins

High-tech/high-return marketing begins with a low-tech/high-sanity mindset. That means comprehending that technology must fit into your marketing and not the other way around.

Technology can be a wild beast that destroys you if you're not in control. So you start out by being in control and you stay in control. You're the boss and technology is the employee.

Guerrilla technology begins with your insight into where low tech touches high tech. You see that the two are very compatible and can help each other if the low tech is in charge. That's why, to get off to the best start with technology, you don't begin with technology.

- Begin with a marketing plan and calendar so that you know where you're going and how you'll get there. Technology will be part of that plan and will help produce many of the marketing weapons on your calendar, but it needs you to call the shots. You do that with a plan and calendar.

- Think in terms of giving things away for free. You are living in the Information Age and it's possible for you to give away a lot of valuable information that will help your prospects and your bottom line.

- Remember that confidence in the seller is the prime attraction to the buyer and that you need all the credibility you can get to earn that confidence. Professional-looking marketing and communications materials give you the credibility you need. And you can create them without paying the price that credibility used to cost.

- Small businesses get a lot of help from their friends in fusion marketing arrangements as we become more interdependent and scratch each others' backs more. Technology makes it easier than ever to connect with others, share leads with others, market with others, render service with others, achieve new profits with others.

- Follow-up is now so easy that it's mandatory if you're serious about turning a consistent profit. Technology lets you save the names of those who deign to do business with you, and stay in touch with them so they know you care. When they do, they'll be a whole lot more likely to do business with you forever. They'll also be a steady supply of referral business, testimonials, and customer data.

 ## Ten technologies that can deliver high returns

Armed with the momentum garnered by standing still a moment, you're now ready to investigate the ten ways that technology can help you satisfy your current customers, convert prospects into customers, energize your profits, and accomplish the equally noble goals of saving your time and being a lot more fun than old-fashioned work.

Are there only ten ways? Of course not. The number is closer to ten times ten, but because we're all so busy these days, I've winnowed it down to ten. Not only that, but I've counted the Internet four times because it serves guerrilla marketers in at least four ways. And I haven't counted many technological breakthroughs because they're not involved enough with marketing. For example, I haven't included video brochures because, although they're high-tech, they're not do-it-yourself technology as these others are. Hey, I know it's an arbitrary list. But it can put you over the top.

Here are the ten high-tech/high-return marketing technologies to notice:

1. Teeming *databases* filled with the names of your customers and prospects enable you to gather a wealth of information about each one of them. This information allows you to establish lasting relationships of mutual value. Obtaining this kind of information is one of the best strategies in marketing, high- or low-tech.

2. The *Internet* provides for communication with e-mail. Its speed and convenience allow businesses to be of better service to their customers and to themselves. You can mail to multitudes with the ease and simplicity of mailing to one. Although we are in the

Information Age we are also in the time-saving age, and e-mail is a way of living in both ages at the same time—or else. If you don't have an e-mail address, expect your prospects and customers to find someone who does, because America is buying things in a new way and that new way is on the Internet.

3. The *Internet* gives access to data. It is an information superlibrary that's bigger every minute, more valuable every hour, better every day, and easier to navigate every week. The value of information is so high and the Internet makes it so easy to access, that businesses operating without this particular library card are like fighters battling with one hand tied behind their backs. You can learn from your industry, peek in on competitors, obtain up-to-the-minute information from all over the world, stay tuned to change as it happens.

4. The *Internet* provides access to people, which is why it is also a communications superhighway. E-mail is just one way to get in touch with people. You can also connect with them in real-time chat situations for some of the most valuable and instant research ever available. Real-time chatting is a powerful marketing tool whether it's one-on-one or in a large online conference. Additionally, you can access people through groups they've joined because of common interests simply by posting messages at no cost, and if your interest dovetails with theirs, they'll probably be delighted to hear from you. You can write and publish your own online column, proving how good you are by the quality of your information, then showing people how to contact you. There are about 50 million people on the Internet now. That's a lot of people you can access.

5. The *Internet* for web marketing may be the most profitable of all the ten technologies, because the web is where people are learning to look for the things they want to buy. As they learned to use the Yellow Pages in the past, they're learning to use the Internet now to search for the best values in the world or in their community. To guerrillas, this represents a stupendous opportunity to talk to targeted prospects who single themselves out by visiting your web site. The site is the right place to give them loads of things to help them succeed. Remember: the best marketing helps prospects to succeed at whatever goal they've selected: earning money, losing weight, finding love, eliminating termites. A winning web site is filled with good information, invites interaction, and stays fresh all the time.

6. A *computer system* for producing marketing materials includes a scanner and color laser printer, along with software that makes producing top-flight marketing weapons a simple and nearly joyous task. I say joyous because it's a whale of a lot of fun to produce highly creative marketing tools after growing up thinking you didn't have a creative bone in your body. It's a gas to produce a first-rate newsletter in a few hours for no money after taking a couple of months and investing a couple thousand bucks to produce a second-rate newsletter in the past.

There are many guerrilla marketing weapons that can be produced by you in your office with your computer. The process of guerrilla marketing is to consider all these weapons, utilize many of them, keep careful track of which are contributing most to your profits, then eliminate the losers and double up on the winners.

Some of these marketing vehicles are musts, such as business cards and envelopes while others are enticing options, such as multimedia presentations and ID cards to members of your frequent buyer club. Open your mind wide and say "ahhhh" as you contemplate the following 27 arenas in which a computer will allow you to operate:

■ Newsletters—Good ones are mailed to customers and prospects on a regular basis, at least quarterly, and they follow the rule of 75/25, meaning give information of worth and value in 75 percent of the newsletter, then sell your products or services—and those of your fusion partners—in 25 percent.

■ Flyers—Also known as circulars, these should be considered all headline, because you've got to make your point in a hurry or not at all. You can distribute them in a variety of ways as well as posting them as signs. Include them in all orders and give them to your fusion marketing partners to distribute for you, just as you distribute theirs.

■ Direct mail letters—You can keep these in your computer, ready to update and personalize at the drop of a beanie. Smart businesses don't wait until the moment they're needed to write letters, but have an inventory of proven-in-action marketing letters in their computers all set to print and mail.

■ Postcards—As much as I believe in the power of direct mail, I admit to favoring postcards, because they take away from the recipient the decision of whether or not to open the envelope. In standard size or oversize six-by-nine-inch format, color postcards are potent door-openers.

■ Letterheads—Guerrilla businesses have a clear identity, which is communicated in their marketing and in their stationery. They're able to produce high-quality stationery at very economical prices using their computer, lowering the cost of doing business in a professional manner.

■ Envelopes—Computers enable small businesses not only to design and produce envelopes that carry forth their identity, but also to assure that the identity is consistent with their other marketing, and that their web site address appears on the

Hello, Techno-Dolly!

Seattle is the home of a genteel place: a museum that celebrates the history and art of dolls. Run as a private, for-profit institution, the museum includes a main gallery (housing its permanent exhibit), a gallery for special exhibits, quiet areas for contemplation and relaxation, and a retail shop. In addition to being open to the general public and for educational tours, the museum is available for receptions and special events.

Despite its whimsical and nostalgic nature, the museum is humming with technology that makes the business run profitably. For example, using technology to bring virtually every marketing function in-house has contributed not only to greater control and cost efficiency but to creativity, flexibility, and collaboration. Desktop publishing software enables the museum to produce a wide variety of professional marketing materials, from gallery opening invitations (including scanned-in slides), to exhibit labels (previously costing up to $20 apiece when outsourced), to membership applications, to advertisements, to facility use guidelines and price lists.

The Internet and e-mail have greatly enhanced the museum store's ability to reach and serve customers. The store can take requests, respond to questions, and fulfill orders electronically. Through its affiliation with the Collectors Direct Network, it offers its entire catalog electronically to the collecting community and takes part in global chat sessions, reinforcing interest in everything the museum has to offer.

envelope. Guerrillas experiment with envelope colors to improve response rates.

■ Business cards—Guerrilla business cards have an individual's name and title, company name, address, phone number, fax number, e-mail address, web site address, logo, and company slogan or theme line, and then probably open up to reveal a list of benefits of doing business with the company or of products and services that the company offers.

■ Invoices—These aren't boring business forms when they're created by a guerrilla marketer. That person recognizes that these are marketing opportunities and prints valuable information on each invoice in addition to the expected names and numbers.

■ Purchase order forms—Computers allow guerrillas not only to produce their own PO forms but also to turn them into semi-brochures for marketing related products and services. All standard office forms are created by guerrillas and transformed into forms plus marketing tools.

■ Brochures—These are high-powered weapons in the hands of guerrillas who realize they are perfect forums for including all the details of their offerings. Guerrillas are so proud of the brochures they create that they often offer them for free in their other marketing, then send them along with a personal note thanking the person for the request. That personal note, coupled with follow-up within a week, results in many brochure requesters becoming paying customers.

■ Catalogs—I know the kind you get in the mail are glossy, thick, and expensive, but yours don't have to be that way—especially expensive. Growing numbers of businesses are enjoying increasing revenues through their catalogs, and now that catalogs are so easy and inexpensive to design and produce, perhaps you should give thought to joining them.

■ Invitations—Guerrillas love to play favorites, their favorites being their best customers, the ones on their A list. They have private sales, parties, and special events, and they print handsome invitations to these gatherings with their computer. It's not quite like printing their own money, but some small business owners feel it comes quite close.

■ Gift certificates—People are often on the lookout for gift ideas and your suggestion of a gift certificate for your product or services might be just the ticket. It costs hardly anything to print up a sign saying "Ask about our gift certificates" or to add that line to an ad, web site, or brochure. But it can become a whole new profit center. Once again, printing these feels like printing cash.

■ Coupons—Computers can print coupons that offer discounts, free merchandise, free services—almost anything to intensify that desire the prospect has for your product. Often a person who is on the fence will leap off it and onto your customer list if motivated by a coupon, especially one with the sense of urgency imparted by a cut-off date. But if you overdo it, your customers will always wait for a bargain and be reluctant to pay full price.

■ Contest entry forms—Many smart small businesses hold contests in order to get names for their mailing lists. If they are retailers, they place the entry boxes in the rear of the store so entrants must walk through and see all the merchandise on their way to entering. Computers enable them to design and produce very tempting entry forms.

■ Club ID cards—Increasing numbers of guerrilla marketers are forming frequent-buyer clubs or VIP customer clubs, then sealing their relationship with members by means of an attractive club identification card. They even print member diplomas.

■ Greeting cards—Few members of society are as nostalgic as guerrillas, who always seem to have a ready supply of in-house-created anniversary cards to celebrate the anniversary of their relationships with customers. They also produce thank-you cards, holiday cards, birthday cards—you-name-it cards—because they've learned that the personal bond strengthens the business bond. The cards are printed by their computer and signed by hand, with a brief personal notation.

- Press releases—Savvy entrepreneurs have learned that when it comes to PR, the media needs them as much as they need the media, as long as the entrepreneurs have real news to offer. Their computer-generated press release forms present news in the formats the media appreciates, often resulting in free publicity.

- Signs—Because so many cities and towns now have community bulletin boards, guerrillas are certain to have their signs posted on those boards constantly. They realize they are reaching prime prospects very economically with this increasingly popular way to market.

- Point-of-purchase materials—Because guerrillas know that nearly three-quarters of purchase decisions are made right at the place of purchase, they are quick to produce POP materials that tie in with their other marketing and generate impulse decisions to buy.

- Trade show materials—Guerrillas know that trade shows represent the second largest marketing expenditure in the nation, trailing only magazine ads, and that they account for 18 percent of marketing budgets. So they create, design, and produce compelling graphic presentations of their sales stories, in a variety of formats, strictly for use at trade shows.

- Audiovisual aids—Top marketers know that points made to the eye are 78 percent more effective than points made to the ear, so they prepare audiovisual support for their presentations. These take the form of diagrams, before-and-after photos, illustrations, product demonstrations—almost anything to help prospects understand how they can benefit by purchasing. Marketers enlist the aid of computers to produce these weapons.

■ Flipcharts—These versatile marketing weapons have audiovisual aids built right into them, present your sales story with an order and a flow, and are powerful sales closers in the hands of even a non-salesperson. Flipcharts are flexible, portable, and now more economical than ever.

■ Research questionnaires—The most sage of all guerrillas prepare these at the outset of their marketing program so they can compile gobs of significant data about their customers, to empower their future efforts at finding people who fit their customer profile. Computers not only design and print the questionnaires but also help store and analyze the data.

■ Books and booklets—People seem to trust published writers, and that's why many small business owners write and self-publish booklets and books. I did. And I didn't have a computer to make it fast, inexpensive, and simple. Still, it worked out exceptionally well for me. Your computer can help see that everything works out even better for you.

■ Proposals—It's at proposal time that the rubber meets the road and a professional presentation of the benefits you offer will pay off the most. Computer-produced proposals add credibility, visibility, and excitement, while instilling confidence in you, something that is beyond any price tag.

■ Multimedia presentations—What were once complicated, troublesome, high-powered, and glamorous are now simple, hassle-free, high-powered, and glamorous. Multimedia presentations, once viewed as invitations to disaster, are now viewed as requisites for success. They allow you to demonstrate clearly the benefits you offer while proving beyond words that you're comfortable with technology.

7. A computer for *networking* gives you an invaluable opportunity to share, to enlist the aid of others, to fusion market, to team up with others not near you. When you can share by networking you can reduce costs, increase productivity, improve customer service, cut down on paperwork, save time, eliminate meeting time, and gain flexibility.

8. A *fax* for communicating is still essential. Although e-mail is becoming more and more popular, the primary method of business communications in offices today remains the facsimile machine. It enables you to transmit documents and graphics in what used to seem like an instant—although compared with the speed of e-mail, it now seems like an eon.

9. *Fax on demand* is the ideal marketing technology in an age when, for many people, instant gratification is not quite fast enough. These people want to call your toll-free number and receive a fax of your brochure or price list before they hang up, and you'd better be prepared to serve them because they know their time is too valuable to waste.

10. *Cellular telephones* enable you to stay in touch with associates and customers, and combination cellular phone/pager/two-way radios that grant you access to the Internet make you even more connected. This technology is a boon to you if your business depends on superlative customer service.

Although the ten technologies I've just examined offer priceless results, they are not high-priced. Always keep in the forefront of your mind that if you don't embrace them, there's a very good chance your competitors will.

Even when you've made these technologies valued members of your marketing team, keep your eyes peeled for new technologies that will add oomph to your marketing. They're coming down the techno-pike a mile a minute, dropping in price as they arrive. Some people ignore them. Others are frightened by them. Guerrillas are fascinated by them. There will be a direct correlation between your fascination with the beauty of these technologies and your fascination with the beauty of your bottom line.

chapter 10

The Glowing Future for Small Business

About four thousand years ago, when the whole idea of individual enterprise began to spread like wildflowers across the planet, all businesses were small businesses. Some of them wanted to remain small businesses. Others wanted to become big businesses. Many were happy just to stay in business. All were limited by the technology of the day.

From 2000 B.C. until very close to A.D. 2000, a lot of well-managed, right-thinking small businesses either failed or they achieved only a portion of the profits they could have earned, a fraction of the excellence of which they were capable. They did the very best they could, but they fell woefully short of their true capabilities.

Then something miraculous happened to propel them forward, to grant them more time than the clock or calendar had previously allowed them, to help them attain the potential that earlier had been out of their grasp.

The incredible explosion

As the twentieth century drew to a close, technology exploded—and it's still exploding. Research done earlier in the century has begun paying off big-time. Sure, there was technology back in the eighteenth and nineteenth centuries, and it brought about the Industrial Revolution. But there's been a quantum leap in technology in the late twentieth century, and instead of favoring huge companies with mass production capabilities, it's helping small businesses unleash their full potential, dramatically increase their profits, and provide their customers with unsurpassed excellence of product and service. Because of the explosive growth of small business, governments and large businesses are becoming more accommodating to small businesses, illuminating their future with promise as never before.

Through the millennia the rules of business have changed. But they're changing now more and faster than ever.

 ## Revolutions all around us

Small business has everything going for it in a world smack dab in the middle of at least ten revolutions at the same time. Actually there are far more than ten, especially in the United States, including revolutions in medicine, space exploration, and transportation. But the future of small business seems to have been impacted by ten in particular:

1. The *technology revolution,* also known as the digital or wireless or computer revolution, provides the Davids of the world with high-tech slingshots with which to do battle against the Goliaths. Mom-and-pop operations are now run by entrepreneurs with the power of Mother Nature and Father Time. The best location in town, the Internet, is affordable by one and all. How long will this revolution continue? Forever is a good guess. If you've recently started a small business, congratulations on your timing.

2. The *time revolution* gives everyone not only a new awareness of time but, more importantly, an awareness of how rare and precious it is. People are discovering that they have less time, as workweeks increase and leisure time decreases. The future of small business is one that grants more time, thanks to the combination of the technology revolution, which enables us to save time, and the time revolution, which teaches us to place a higher priority on that time.

3. The *psychology revolution* allows us to discard notions about people that have never been proven and adjust our attitudes and actions to accommodate those which have. New findings about human behavior are constantly being reported to the public and the public is responding with a new sense of self-awareness, a new striving toward self-improvement, a new self-esteem that motivates more education, better learning, greater skills, and a more evolved attitude. We are learning why people buy, why they don't buy, what business practices turn them off and which turn them on. We're learning that they ignore businesses that ignore them and recommend businesses that pay personal attention to them.

4. The *information revolution* gets much press these days. That's because there is a greater wealth of information now than ever, because information keeps increasing exponentially, and because information is accessible to more people than ever. The Internet, still a baby, is the greatest source of information in history, and the human babies of today are learning to use it to gain access to data at the same time as their teachers are learning to use it to teach more effectively than ever.

5. The *love revolution* in business is just beginning but will continue well into the next century, if, indeed, it ever ends. Love is developing in relationships between businesses and customers, businesses and suppliers, businesses and employees, businesses and other businesses. In addition, the number of couples working together at home is increasing. The irony is that technology, thought to be cold and impersonal, is really allowing people to cozy up to each other, relate, grow close, be warm, be human.

6. The *consciousness revolution* is the underlying reason behind the time revolution and the love revolution. It leads people to strive to call their own shots, pull their own strings, be in charge of their own destinies, and to embrace the technology that helps them to do so— technology they once feared. It is a guiding force behind the entire movement toward small business. As we see the workaholics among us, our consciousness makes us realize that these people are as sick as any addict, and our consciousness spurs us to value all the more our precious personal time.

7. The *education revolution* is dramatically increasing the quality of education. Computers are being employed to be sure, and the Internet is being accessed. But in addition, schools are learning that nonassigned seating increases attention and that allowing kids to speak to each other instead of passing notes to each other reduces behavior problems. Educators are discovering that cutting down on homework increases the effectiveness of teachers as well as the quality of life for children. Smaller classes, more individualized attention, and increased use of technology are allowing educators to succeed at the true purpose of schooling, which is less to teach than to get children to love learning.

8. The *connectivity revolution* is underway, with a force and energy that is changing the entire world. People are connecting with each other at in-person community functions, and at work via telephones, pagers, fax machines, the Internet, networked computers, chat rooms, and video conferencing. New infrastructures for communication are constantly being built and improved by phone companies, cable firms, technology businesses, and media conglomerates. The word virtual has come to mean connected, as technology makes it easier than ever to hook up with others in a quest for mutual success and satisfaction. The benefits of collaboration are becoming more apparent as the media discovers and reports on them. Is the connectivity revolution akin to the communications revolution? They're one and the same, because the main purpose of connecting is communicating.

9. The *work revolution* is the one you're involved in right now, thanks to technology that allows your small business to compete with much bigger ones. This revolution is making itself known at the workplace and at home, but especially in the elimination of the lines between the two. Small businesses are growing. Home-based businesses are growing. Start-up businesses are growing. What isn't growing is the number of employees at giant companies. Many of them have been downsized out of a job and into a life as an entrepreneur. Again, technology is fueling this revolution, creating, through such means as the Internet, a fertile breeding ground for new companies, new jobs, and new work opportunities.

10. The *candor revolution* is asserting itself among a public that is tired of playing phony games and longs for honesty, disclosure, and revelation. Candor is the theme of the times, as new issues come into the open in literature, politics, entertainment, business, and the media. This candor is a safeguard against mythology that is counterproductive to evolution. It's the great equalizer between people not considered equal in the past. It separates the real world from the dream world and enables society to vent its anxieties and get on with the business of reality. It also allows people to see big business and full-time employment in a new context, held up to the light of small business and less-than-full-time employment. Judging by the growth of small business, it appears people are getting a new message. That message is that the time has never been better to establish, operate, and succeed with a small business.

Smallness over bigness

Because of these simultaneous revolutions, none expected to peter out in the near future, the environment favors smallness over bigness, individuality over depersonalization. It favors the guerrilla without the money who is willing to invest the time, over the non-guerrilla with the money who is not willing to invest the time.

The future economy favors three areas in which small businesses have an almost automatic edge: flexibility, customer service, and personalization. It belongs to companies that can act like small businesses in these areas, regardless of their size.

Increasing your comfort level

The future of small business will glow in direct proportion to the comfort level business owners can achieve with so much change going on. You must be comfortable with technology because the revolution will go on whether or not you are part of it, and if you're comfy and cozy you'll be able to tap into the power and momentum of technological advancements that can put your company into a hyperprofit mode. If you're hazy about the technology, intimidated by it, or planning to avoid it, you've got three strikes against you before you step up to the plate.

You've got to remember that nobody was born with technological enlightenment. Everybody who has it had to learn it. And the best time to learn it is immediately. The longer you are involved with it, the greater your comfort level.

The fortunes amassed by companies in technology are coming from products and services that didn't even exist a decade ago. More than half of the revenues earned by Silicon

Valley technology companies in 1997 come from products that didn't even exist two years earlier. Even the largest and most sophisticated companies of the Fortune 500 can't have used computer technology or been involved with the Internet longer than many small business owners.

In 1984, hardly the Dark Ages, the average product development cycle was three years. By 1990 it had sped up to 18 months. In 1997 it is six months. And it's getting shorter. New products are being introduced lightning fast, and the successful small business owner of the future will not be the one who learns everything but the one who learns one thing after another.

Your comfort level with technology must be equaled by your grace and ability to function in a society with a different awareness of time, a deeper understanding of people, more top-quality information, greater love, a higher consciousness overall, a more pertinent education, closer connections to allies, a more effective way to work, and a more open and honest approach to everything. If you're not comfortable with these changes, you'll have trouble dealing with a public that is.

Being able to operate your computer's word processing program is one thing. Being able to resonate with a real person on a one-to-one basis is something else entirely.

 ## Heads and tails at the same time

The future of small business will be controlled by those business owners who are skilled in contrasting areas:

- They must be able to communicate with large numbers of people.
  at the same time . . .
  They must be able to communicate one-on-one.

- They must excel at writing because of more electronic networking.
  at the same time . . .
  They must excel at speaking because of more in-person networking.

- They must be superb with the broad strokes of strategic planning.
    at the same time . . .
  They must be superb with the crucial details of running a business.

- They must be at home with the futuristic values of speed and candor.
    at the same time . . .
  They must be at home with the traditional values of patience and love.

- They must be aggressive in competing, with an eye toward profits.
    at the same time . . .
  They must be aggressive in collaborating, with an eye toward profits.

- They must offer the credibility and professionalism of a big business.
    at the same time . . .
  They must offer the warmth and personal touch of a small business.

- They must have a zealous commitment to their established marketing.
    at the same time . . .
  They must keep an eagle eye for innovation and trends.

- They must be able to act without worrying about what others think.
    at the same time . . .
  They must be able to act with acute sensitivity to what others feel.

- They must be able to grow and expand without sacrificing profitability.
    at the same time . . .
  They must be able to profit and flourish without sacrificing humanity.

■ They must be outstanding in their own field no matter what it is.

   at the same time . . .

They must be outstanding in marketing, for everything must be sold.

As voluntary as a thumb

Is technology really mandatory for small business now and in the future? Not really—if you think a thumb isn't mandatory for a hand to do its thing properly.

It used to be that a computer was considered a luxury. And in the same way, I guess my puppy would consider a thumb on his paw to be a luxury. But computers—and the ability to get the most out of them—have become compulsory equipment for guerrillas. Guerrillas are so tuned into technology that "upgrade" is their middle name. They don't hold back but instead invest in the best technology available today and know they can upgrade later.

Saving money skydiving

As a guerrilla wouldn't have saving money as his or her prime motivation in purchasing equipment for an ocean dive or a skydive, that same guerrilla knows that forsaking quality to save money in the purchase of business equipment is often a false economy. By viewing the cost of technology as an investment rather than an expense, guerrillas are able to live in the present, escape from the past, and prepare for the future. They've seen how the right technology has a short payoff time and how it can help generate profits that make the business owner wonder why he waited so long to invest in the first place.

They never invest in technology just because they think they should. They invest in it because they need it and they know just how they can use it. They invest because they don't want their competitors to have an edge over them granted by better technology.

 ## The miniaturization of America

The biggest part of the American economy is small business. The fastest growing segment of the American economy is small business. The greatest number of employees in America are employed by small business.

Businesses are getting smaller. Families are getting smaller. Computers are getting smaller. Even big corporations are getting smaller. Downsizing, described by some as an economic drive-by shooting, has made the big guys smaller while forcing many once bored employees into becoming thriving and excited entrepreneurs. They've discovered fulfillment and success in circumstances they thought were bad but turned out to be glorious.

For a reason unknown to all but the dinosaurs, small business, especially from the forties to the nineties, thought that its prime mission was to get large. But the more this passion was put into practice the more it weighed down small businesses, strangling both the enterprise, with a dearth of profits, and the owner, with a surfeit of new problems caused by swimming in uncharted, shark-filled waters that were over his or her head to begin with.

It wasn't until very recently that small business came to its senses and realized that big does not automatically mean successful and that expansion is not always a blessing. Diversification and gigantism are giving way to focus and precision.

Instead of using technology to free up time for the business owner to engage in more work, guerrillas are using technology to free up time for themselves to engage in things other than work. Their plans aren't necessarily smaller. They are just more humane, more evolved.

The goals of small business

The goals of small business are to establish as many relationships and render the best service possible, not simply to grow and make as many sales as possible, though increasing profitability will always be a goal. The goals of future small business will be to create an environment in which the journey is every bit as pleasant and rewarding as the destination, and to set up a company that is durable, flexible, and interdependent, yet self-sufficient. Rather than pursuing the goals of our ancestors, small businesses today are pursuing goals that are in accordance with their newly reexamined priorities.

 ## New priorities for new times

Glowing, increasing, substantial profits are not to be undervalued. But your family and friends are more important than profits any day. Now that you know that time is not money, and that it is far more valuable than money, it should come as zero surprise to you that free time is a priority—free time to spend in your own recreational pursuits, to be with your family and friends.

Many small business owners place the pursuit and attainment of excellence as their top priority. I like to do business with these people because, like everyone else, I'm drawn to the best and I want to patronize the best. It's not too hard to tell which businesses are out for the most money and which are out to do and be the best.

Naturally, good health is a high priority, and along with it, the longevity that undoubtedly comes from fitness, fulfillment, creativity, and self-expression. The revolution in medicine will allow our extra years to be characterized by sparkling health.

 ## The thrill of a challenge

A crucial goal of small businesses will always be to experience the thrill of challenge. It is the meeting and surmounting of challenge that energizes passion, and it is passion that makes business profitable. The best small business owners are the most passionate. They are passionate about their business, their customers, their excellence, and their success. Their passion shows through with their service and quality.

The entrepreneurs of today seek to love their work. Being guerrillas, they are cognizant that the journey should be the goal, so they look forward to their work on a daily basis.

The small business owners of today have no problem with using the word fun. They want their work to be fun, and they've structured it to be fun. They know that winning is a lot more fun than losing, so they've positioned themselves to win, to profit, to succeed at achieving their goals.

The newest priority, although it stems from age-old enlightenment, is balance: between work and leisure; between getting bigger and getting better; between becoming wealthy with money and becoming wealthy with fulfillment. Guerrillas strive for balance above all, knowing it is the most difficult to attain and the most rewarding over time.

 Homework up ahead

Much of the future of small business will take place in a location you can commute to in your slippers—your home office. Studies by the Small Business Administration show that 95 percent of home businesses make a profit the first year.

But profit doesn't seem to be the only pot of gold at the end of the rainbow. A survey by *Income Opportunities* magazine reported that 94 percent of home business owners say they enjoy working from home most of the time, and 63 percent like it all of the time. One of the things many of them relish is the equivalent of an extra decade granted to their lives by freedom from commuting. Another popular benefit is control over their work schedule so that they can care for their kids themselves and not turn them over to child care by others.

The U.S. Department of Transportation tells us that in 1992 there were 2.3 million telecommuters, and by 2002 there will be 15 million. That's a chunky 650 percent increase in ten years. Sounds like a lot more kids in the future will be with their parents during those crucial formative years.

Between 1991 and 1996, the number of full- and part-time home workers in the U.S. grew from 26 million to over 40 million, according to IDC/Link, a research and consulting firm. That number is increasing with each sentence I enter into my word processor. It's predicted to rise as high as 75 million during the year 2000.

Hmmm, that sure sounds like a glowing future for small business to me. I've been working from my home, living in that future and loving it, since 1971. That's a lot of time to amass regrets but I can't think of even one.

The starting point

Here I am bursting with all this good news about technology and its ability to shorten your workweek and increase your leisure, but at the same time I want you to know that this can only be part of your future if you're a small business. Technology is not shortening the workweek for big business employees. In spite of the widespread reverberations of the technology explosion, the average employee of a multinational corporation in 1996 worked 20 percent more hours and slept 20 percent fewer than he or she did in 1986. That's because the best place for technology to work its time-saving and freedom-granting wonders is in a small business. And the starting point is in the mind of the small business owner who creates a plan with time and freedom at its core.

Those big corporations that are asking for more work from their employees have a whale of a lot of advanced technology. You can be certain of that. But they don't have the mindset of saving time for their employees to use for living rather than earning a living. When you're directing your own show, you'd never deprive yourself of the freedom to be yourself, would you?

Technology can help your business in many ways, from freeing you from boring detail work to empowering your marketing. But it's you who will call the shots, you who will determine what to do with your extra time and money. Your job is to remember that technology is a tool and not a master, that it should be more about people than about things, and that its greatest contributions will be made to places within you, and not limited to your bottom line.

 ## Fitting into the future

Woody Allen once said that a nuclear holocaust isn't all that bad if you're dressed for it. And I'm here to say that the technology explosion is going to be absolutely wonderful for you— if you're dressed for it. You've got to dress your business with the proper technology of the day and prepare yourself and your employees, your allies and your suppliers, to ride the crests of today's multiple revolutions rather than trying to swim against the tide.

The tide is carrying the wave of technology toward you so fast that an innovation in digital technology is copyrighted worldwide every three seconds. It's not a future you can hide from.

You may pick up a book at a bookstore and learn secrets that you hope your competitors never learn. But they know all about the revolutions, especially the one concerning technology, and they're doing everything they can to outsmart you, outmarket you, outservice you, and outperform you. Many of them can outspend you. But can they outthink you?

Not if you're all set for the future. Not if you're geared up to capitalize upon the momentum that has already been achieved. If you're a small business, or even planning to start one, you've got everything going for you now. The future favors small business. Armed with the right equipment and enlightened by the right attitude, you ought to be glowing as brightly as that future.

Glossary of Key Terms

Application: A software package that performs a particular service, such as e-mail or providing access to data on the World Wide Web.

Browser: A program used to access and view information on the World Wide Web.

Client/Server Network: A hierarchical computer system in which "clients" (standard desktop PCs or workstations) are connected by cable to a centralized, more powerful computer that "serves up" data, software, and applications.

Bulletin Board System (BBS): Any computer system and software with phone lines that will accept a phone call from another computer with little or no prior arrangement for making access. People with similar interests join these systems.

Chat Room: An area in an online service where several users can meet simultaneously in real time and exchange typed messages.

Conference: A large chat room session that usually features a main speaker and an audience that asks questions.

Cyberspace: A name for the online world.

Discussion Group: An electronic message board on an online service, a BBS, or the Internet. The board contains messages focusing on a specific topic.

Domain Name: An entry in an Internet address, such as microsoft.com. In the United States, common domain names end with .com (for commercial organizations), .org (for organizations), .net (for network providers), .gov (for government), and .mil (for military). In other countries, two-letter codes represent each country, for example: .fr for France, .de for Germany, .uk for the United Kingdom, .ca for Canada, and .jp for Japan.

Download: To retrieve a file from an online service, a BBS, or an Internet server, or from e-mail.

E-commerce: Electronic commerce. The process of buying and selling over the web.

E-mail: A means of exchanging typed messages between computer users in which messages are sent to specific addresses and stored in mailboxes. E-mail is currently the most popular activity of people online.

Extranet: Use of Internet standards, technologies, and products to link an enterprise collaboratively with its network of customers, suppliers, and distributors. Access is limited to members of the extended community.

FAQ (Frequently Asked Questions): Usually a document containing questions and answers that address the basics of a subject. A visitor can find an FAQ on almost every web site. An FAQ serves to introduce a visitor to the topic or subject of the web site and to offer general guidelines about how to best use the site.

Flame: To send a poison-pen e-mail to another Internet user. Sometimes senders of unwanted e-mail get flamed by recipients.

GIF (Graphics Interchange Format): A computer graphics file format developed for use in photo-quality graphic image display on computer screens. Now commonly used on the Internet.

Home Page: The page that serves as the starting point of a World Wide Web site, sometimes named default.html or index.html. It usually contains the site's name and a directory of its contents.

Host: Any computer that provides services to remote computer users.

Hot Link: A connection to a document or other file on the Internet that generally appears as a highlighted word, usually in blue, or an image on the screen. Also Hypertext Link or Link.

HTML (Hypertext Markup Language): A language used to format documents that can then be interpreted and rendered by an Internet browser, usually on the World Wide Web. Such documents can also be rendered on a local computer or internal network by a browser.

HTTP (Hypertext Transfer Protocol): A basic communication protocol for Internet or web server file input and output.

Hypertext: A type of database system in which objects (text, pictures, music, programs, and so on) can be creatively linked to each other. Usually written in HTML, hypertext systems are particularly useful for organizing and navigating through large databases that consist of disparate types of information.

Interface: The point at which a connection is made between two elements so they can work with one another.

Internet: Abbreviation for Internetwork. A set of dissimilar computer networks joined together by gateways that handle data transfer and convert messages from the sending network to receiving networks. Originally part of the Department of Defense's Advanced Research Project Administration.

Intranet: Use of Internet standards, technologies, and products within an enterprise to function as a collaborative processing infrastructure. The term Intranet is generally used to describe the application of Internet technologies to internal corporate networks.

ISDN (Integrated Services Digital Network): An emerging technology offered by most telephone service providers as a faster alternative to traditional modems. ISDN combines voice and digital network services in a single medium, making it possible to offer telephone customers digital data service and voice connection through a single "wire."

ISP (Internet Service Provider): An organization that provides access to the Internet, usually for a fee.

Mailbot: A type of program that responds automatically to incoming e-mail. It recognizes key words and replies to the people who use them. This is also called an auto-responder.

Menu: A set of choices presented to you on a computer monitor.

Modem: A shortening of the words "*mo*dulator *dem*odulator." A device that allows a computer to connect with other computers over standard telephone lines by dialing phone numbers. Current modems use telephone lines, which make them relatively slower than upcoming modems, which use cable fiber-optic wiring or satellite technology.

Multitasking: The ability to simultaneously execute multiple applications within an operating system.

Net: The Net is the Internet as Netizens are the people who use it and Netiquette is the unwritten code of proper online behavior. It's all part of the new techno-slang centering on the Internet.

Networking: Individual computers connecting by means of a host computer so that all may share information and resources.

Newsgroup: A discussion group or exchange of information on the Internet that focuses on a particular subject.

Online Service: A large commercial bulletin board system that accommodates hundreds or thousands of users at once, offers a wide variety of services and information, and charges a monthly subscription fee. The most widely used online services presently are America Online, Microsoft Network, CompuServe, and Prodigy.

Search Engine: A site on the World Wide Web that serves as a comprehensive searchable index of web sites, typically by scanning the web for key words.

Server: A computer running administrative software that controls access to all or part of a network and its resources.

Site: A specific location on the Internet.

Snail Mail: An onliner's term for standard postal mail. E-mail is now more commonly used than snail mail and the U.S. Postal Service uses e-mail. The name refers to the relative speed of paper mail.

Storefront: A location on the web. An online service or a bulletin board that stores a collection of information about your business which can be accessed by others at any time. The primary purpose of a storefront is e-commerce.

Upload: To transfer a file from a computer to a BBS, an online service, or a server on the Net.

URL (Uniform [or Universal] Resource Locator): An address that uniquely identifies a World Wide Web site, usually preceded with http:// such as in this fictitious URL: http://www.example.microsoft.com/.

Web: The World Wide Web, which is one part of the Internet.

Web Site: A home page located on the Internet.

World Wide Web: Also the web or WWW. A set of services that run on top of the Internet providing a cost-effective way of publishing information, supporting collaboration and work-flow, and delivering business applications to any connected user in the world. The web is a collection of Internet host systems that make these services available on the Internet using the HTTP.

Zine: An electronic publication on one very specific topic, published by one person or a handful of people, and distributed for free at intervals online. Adapted from the print media term "magazine."

Resources

STEP-BY-STEP START-UP GUIDES:

How to Select or
Upgrade a Personal Computer . . . **157**

How to Save Money by
Sharing Files, Printers, and More . . . **163**

How to Create and Deliver a Newsletter . . . **167**

How to Create Brochures and Flyers . . . **173**

How to Conduct Business
Research on the Internet . . . **177**

How to Create a Simple Web Page . . . **181**

55 TECHNOLOGY TIPS . . . **187**

WHAT'S YOUR TECHFICIENCY QUOTIENT? . . . **199**

Appendix materials have been adapted from the following sources: Start-Up Guides were adapted from Microsoft Corporation's series of informational "How to . . ." brochures, 1997 (also published on Microsoft's Small Business web site); "55 Technology Tips" and the "What's Your Techficiency Quotient?" quiz were adapted from the Microsoft Small Business Council brochure, "101 Technology Tips for Managing a Successful Small Business," 1997.

How to Select or Upgrade a Personal Computer

Maybe you're ready to purchase your first computer because you realize that automating manual tasks can help you refocus on the reasons you went into business in the first place. With rapidly advancing technology and a wide variety of price and performance options available, you can find the solution that's right for your business.

Or does the personal computer you have seem slow lately? Do you want to use time-saving new software applications but lack enough memory? If you can't afford to buy a new system, consider upgrading your PC. Upgrading your computer's memory, processor, and hard disk can boost your PC's performance—and your productivity.

Put terminology such as RAM, megahertz, and gigabytes aside for a moment. The only reason to buy or upgrade a computer is to accomplish more tasks faster. Simplify by starting with defining what you want to do.

Would you like to keep track of product inventory? Publish flyers or newsletters? Research or sell products on the Internet? Each of these tasks can be accomplished on your PC with the right software. So the best place to start is to identify the software programs you want to run and then choose the right PC or upgrades.

step 1 Choose a computer system appropriate to your needs

Many manufacturers now make your task of choosing the right computer easier by creating systems designed for small businesses. These PCs provide small businesses with the right amount of performance, without too many bells and whistles. They generally come with an operating system (on which to run software programs) and set of business-oriented programs already installed.

For a new system, expect to spend between $1,700 and $3,500, depending on your needs. PC upgrade options start as low as $100. As you make your decision concerning hardware and operating system, keep in mind the capabilities you want your system to have, such as:

- running many different programs (e.g., desktop publishing, financial spreadsheets and inventory control, relational databases, graphics)

- remote computing (reaching your computer or network from another location using a modem)

- multitasking

- e-mail and Internet access

- network security and reliability

step 2 Maximize speed and memory performance

First and foremost, buy or upgrade to the fastest processor and the most memory (RAM, or random access memory) you can afford. If you are buying new, find a system with:

- 166-megahertz (MHz) or 200-MHz processor

- 16 to 32 megabytes (MB) of RAM

Upgrading a processor can be as simple as removing the old chip and plugging in a new, faster chip. You can currently upgrade a 386 to a 486 for about $99, or a 486 to a P5 (a very fast processor) for around $175.

RAM upgrades are especially reasonable. Expect to spend about $10 per MB of memory. If you've got 8 MB now, that translates to about $80 to get you up to 16 MB or about $240 to get up to 32 MB.

Be careful about upgrade costs. If you only need one or two elements to get the performance you want, it will probably be cheaper to upgrade. But if you need to upgrade in several areas because your system technology is so out of date, it will make more sense to invest in a new PC featuring the most current technology.

step **3** **Expand storage space**

Today's powerful new software applications and large graphics files available from the Internet require increasingly more space on your hard disk. Your business will benefit from expanding the space available in your system to handle these storage demands.

For the greatest versatility, consider buying or upgrading your system with:

- large hard disk (about 2.0 GB)

- standard 3.5-inch high-density disk drive

- CD-ROM drive (at least 4X)

Always back up everything before removing the current hard disk, so you won't lose everything already stored there. Cost for a new disk is roughly $200–$400.

External drives are another great option for data storage. There are inexpensive cartridge drives available for backing up your important business files on disks that hold upward of 100 MB. These large-capacity disks make daily backup feasible and simple. And you can transport your stored files to other holding areas or workstations, making it easy to share documents that can't fit on a regular 3.5-inch diskette.

step **4** **Communicate with all-in-one fax/data/voice**

Modems enable you to transfer data over telephone lines. Using a modem and the right software you can:

- use your computer to send and receive faxes and e-mail

- access your computer from a remote location

- connect to the Internet

Using your fax/modem to send and receive faxes gives you more flexibility. For example, you can program it to send a fax at a time convenient for a client, and you can manipulate and store received fax data electronically, so you don't waste expensive fax paper.

As with PCs in general, look for the highest modem performance you can afford, as speed (measured in kilobytes per second, or Kbps) dramatically affects the rate of transfer of information, which affects your telephone costs.

Although slower modems can adequately handle transferring text such as regular e-mail (without attached files), you want a high-speed modem (at least 28.8 Kbps) for faster Internet access. A fast modem is especially valuable if you need to download or transfer pictures or graphics files.

The 28.8 Kbps modems start at around $100. You can spend up to $400 for modems with telephone headset, speakerphone, and voice mail capabilities, which enable you to use your modem and computer as your telephone and answering machine. Check with your vendor to ensure that your software allows you to perform all the tasks mentioned above. And stay alert for new high-speed cable modems.

step **5** **Improve your view**

Most systems come standard with a 15-inch monitor. If you spend a lot of time at the computer or will have multiple documents and applications open at the same time, it's worthwhile to upgrade to a larger monitor. The 17-inch monitor has roughly 30 percent more viewing space, which is enough to save you from having to resize windows to see what you're working on.

Using a larger monitor also reduces eyestrain and contributes to your comfort during those extended work periods. To minimize neck strain, be certain the monitor has a tilt/swivel base that allows you to adjust the angle of viewing to the most comfortable position.

The cost for upgrading to the larger monitor ranges from $150 to $300, but spending that extra money can be of immense value to your eyes and your productivity in the long run.

Tips for personal computer shopping

Where you buy your PC or upgrade components depends on how you like to shop. Remember to carefully research all PC brands and suppliers. Also, know your budget and requirements so you get the right system for your business needs. The three basic options are:

Mail order   If you know what you want and are comfortable with terminology and options, mail order typically offers great prices, wide selection, and speedy (even next day) delivery. To order product catalogs, look in computer trade magazines for mail order toll-free phone numbers.

Retailers/Superstores   These are great places to test new products and prospective PCs in the showroom. Most larger cities have several major computer retailers. Many offer special payment options if financing is an issue for your business.

Computer specialty stores or value-added resellers   Also known as system builders and VARs, these companies specialize in assembling computers and are the best places to go if you want your machine customized. Consider this option if you have special needs such as network installation, application design, and training. Check your local directory or contact your software manufacturer for authorized names and locations.

How to Save Money by Sharing Files, Printers, and More

If you are like many small businesses today, you need faster ways to receive, distribute, and manipulate information. And you need to save money on expensive equipment such as color printers, scanners, and CD-ROM drives.

If you have two or more personal computers in your office, you can take a leap in efficiency and productivity by linking your PCs together in a computer network.

Computer networking allows you to share files and documents for better customer, supplier, and employee communications. It reduces duplication of effort, so you get more done in less time, which can gain you a competitive business advantage. It connects everyone in your office so you can promptly meet customer needs. And you can realize productivity gains as employees work together simultaneously on projects. Ultimately, a network also makes the most of expensive printers and peripherals by sharing them and controlling who has access to them.

step **1** **Connect your computers and peripherals**

The most basic network—and an inexpensive solution for companies with fewer than ten computers—is a peer-to-peer network. Peer-to-peer networking offers a quick and easy way to tie all your resources and people together. If you want to connect your office computers, your best bet is to purchase a kit that has all the components and installation instructions packaged together. To do it yourself, here's basically what you'll need:

Network cable Decide if you want to go with coaxial (also called thinnet) cable or RJ45 (also called twisted pair) cable. Coaxial cable is easiest to set up, but if one computer goes down, all the computers in your network go down. With RJ45 cable, you must purchase a hub, which costs $200–$300. But this prevents all the computers in your system from going down if one crashes.

Network cards Next, you'll need to purchase networking cards for each computer to go with the cable you selected. These cards range in price from about $40 to $180.

Installation of these items will be slightly different depending on the computers you own. For more specific instructions on connecting the cards, cables, and computers, follow your manufacturer's operating manual instructions.

step **2** **Develop a file sharing strategy**

To manage your business for maximum efficiency and productivity, you must be able to share, distribute, and manipulate information. Once your computers and peripherals are connected, you can easily begin sharing files and printers.

For example, if you are president of a small real estate firm, you can keep your staff fully informed of your daily schedule by sharing your business calendar. Then you can forget about the hassle of leaving notes about where you can be reached and when you'll return. To give your customers royal treatment, make your customer database available on the network. This way, anyone taking a call can quickly pull up a customer profile to make any needed changes or gain information. And for your monthly sales reports, agents can update reports on their own computers as sales occur, saving you the time and headache of compiling it. You can even have several people working on the same document simultaneously.

step **3** **Share printers and peripherals**

A peer-to-peer network not only saves you time but can also save you money. Valuable tools—such as color and laser printers that allow you to produce professional marketing materials in-house, CD-ROM drives that take advantage of the newest in multimedia applications, and modems that provide access to fax and Internet capabilities—make it possible for the small business to compete on a more level playing field with bigger businesses.

However, these peripherals can be expensive, and acquiring more than you need can drain your resources. Connecting your printers and other peripherals to the network helps stretch your existing resources and reduce outgoing cash flow.

You can connect these devices to the network for use by all employees or only by those who need them. Keep your costs in check both by sharing these resources and by controlling who has access to them.

step **4** **Control network security**

While you do need to ensure that everyone has access to the most current information, you also need to protect your critical files, such as payroll and inventory, from unauthorized access.

Setting permissions on a network allows you to easily share information with those who need to know, while at the same time protecting the same information from those who don't need to know. Unless an employee has specific permission—or knows the password—he or she cannot access inappropriate information on the network.

A tip for the networked office

As you add people and computers, you may want to move to a client/server network to get the network performance you need. A client/server network is a computer system where clients (standard desktop PCs or workstations) are connected by cable to a centralized server. The server is typically a more powerful PC dedicated to "serving up" data, devices, and software to the clients.

How to Create and Deliver a Newsletter

One thing on which the experts agree: follow-up is the most important, yet, perhaps, least-used marketing strategy for small business. A promotional newsletter with trade news, customer stories, and new and interesting information about your business is a great way to help you establish and improve customer relationships.

You don't have to spend a fortune hiring a graphic design firm to create your newsletter or other printed marketing pieces. Today's word processing programs are powerful enough to handle more than just business correspondence. With the right tools and some general guidelines, you can produce your own newsletters at a fraction of the cost of paying someone else to do it.

step **1** **Develop a clear objective**

To ensure that your publication will be cost effective and have as much impact as possible, determine the primary purpose of your newsletter. You might choose to focus on updates—information on new products and latest offers. Or perhaps you want to build familiarity with your company, with articles featuring employees and internal processes. Another effective strategy is to provide "value-added" information that relates to your business, such as technical advice, tips on industry trends, and information regarding legal regulation.

After you've determined your purpose, create regular departments that will give your newsletter a consistent look and complement your feature story or stories. These departments let readers know what to expect.

Possible features include:

- letter from the editor (or company president)

- question-and-answer section

- calendar of events

- special offers or coupons

- humor, anecdotes, quotations, or side notes related to your business

Once you've determined your objective and basic features, you are ready to focus on design.

step **2** Build eye-catching designs

Good design helps get your message across. Of course, design sense is not developed overnight, and it is not the intent here to offer a crash course in graphic design. Experiment and seek out feedback from colleagues, associates, and customers. Many word processing and desktop publishing programs come equipped with design templates to get you started, and you can eventually establish your own templates.

Some features to keep in mind as you begin to design:

Typeface Gothic? Modern? Classic? Jazzy? The style reflects your newsletter's objectives and helps establish your customers' perceptions. Is the newsletter intended to be playful? Entertaining? Informative? Authoritative?

Number of columns Determining the number of columns per page affects the relative openness of the newsletter's design and should be appropriate for the length of articles or other features.

Elements   There are a variety of text elements that provide vital information while serving to enhance the design, such as table of contents, date, volume and issue numbers, and headlines.

Keep in mind that your newsletter should be eye-catching but simple. Use only a couple of easy-to-read typefaces and only enough visual elements to generate interest without looking cluttered.

step **3** **Focus on relevant content**

As well as promoting your products and services, your newsletter can improve customer relations by providing information that is valuable to your clients. Add question-and-answer columns, market statistics and trends, technical advice, or how-to sections.

Think like the customer   When planning stories, ask yourself, "If I were the customer, what information would be most interesting to me?" Write with an informative tone, rather than using the hard sell approach.

Include a tag line   State your mission in a tag line that tells who you are and what you do. If your publication is passed on to readers who don't know you, this will introduce you to new prospects.

Consult the World Wide Web   Use the web to tap into industry data, to import maps, and to search out a wide variety of information that can be incorporated as newsletter content.

Between publications, look for information that would enhance your newsletter. Type content into separate documents as you find time, and import them into your newsletter template at publishing time.

step **4** **Define your layout**

A few well-placed graphics, pictures, sidebars, and pull quotes give your newsletter a polished look. Use these elements to draw the reader's eye and break up big blocks of text. But be selective. Keep it simple.

Add graphics, photos, and clip art These can be scanned from other printed materials or accessed over the web. Be aware that for some images you will need to secure permission for reproduction.

Import spreadsheets and charts Give the customer informative charts and data imported directly from spreadsheets and graphics files.

Use pull quotes and sidebars Call the reader's attention to the most important information in an article, or enhance or break up the main text with case examples, anecdotes, and other elements set off by boxes, different typefaces, or shading.

step **5** **Reach the right people**

To get your newsletters to all the right customers, keep an updated list of customer names and addresses in a single spreadsheet, word processing, or database file. Create mailing labels directly from this database. You can also save money by eliminating the need for an envelope. Save a place on your newsletter for a mailing label and postage—then simply fold, attach, and mail. Ask your local post office for bulk mail rates and requirements.

Publish and distribute your newsletter quarterly or every other month to keep customer awareness high. It is better to start with a less frequent schedule than to get several months into it and realize you don't have enough time or input to publish monthly.

Tips for effective newsletters

Here are a couple of additional ideas for helping you go that extra mile in creating a winning newsletter.

Get your audience involved   Encourage customer feedback by asking for response. Give them plenty of chances to contact you: include your address, phone and fax numbers, and e-mail and web site addresses. Consider adding a clip-and-return survey, calendar of events, or savings coupon. Reach out to your customers and they'll know you are interested in them.

Personalize the newsletter with customer faces and names
Most people are thrilled to see their names in print. Use your customer names, ideas, stories, and pictures in the newsletter. But be sure to get permission before you use this information.

How to Create Brochures and Flyers

Printed marketing materials play a critical role in your marketing plan and your success in selling your products and services. Thoughtfully planned, well designed brochures and flyers can do much of your marketing legwork for you.

Brochures can introduce you to prospective customers and tell your story. They provide potential clients with more information than you can give over the phone or in a short meeting. They help you follow up with customers and enhance your overall identity.

A flyer—printed on one side of a letter-size sheet—is the easiest-to-produce, least expensive marketing tool available. Mail it, hand it out, and leave it wherever prospects might see it to draw attention to your business.

step 1 Craft a benefit-oriented message

For the greatest impact, the primary focus of your marketing materials should be how your organization benefits the customer. This will help gain interest and personalize your product or service.

Tell customers how they will benefit by choosing your products and services. Show them specific examples of how you provide these benefits for current customers. Be positive, yet always be honest. Outrageous claims will turn people away.

Emphasize your benefits in the most-often-read places. No matter how exciting your brochure or flyer is, few prospects will read every word. The most attention-getting spots in a brochure include:

- front cover

- headlines

- subheads

- pull quotes

- sidebars

- captions

Because a flyer is usually on a single sheet, be even more specific and selective about the information you include than in your brochure. Sum up your most important message in a single sentence, and highlight this tag line in boldface or larger type.

step **2** Create a call to action

In addition to informing customers and potential customers, effective brochures and flyers involve the customer and encourage participation or action. They can entice people to inquire about your business or even try what you have to offer.

Tell the reader exactly what you want them to do. No need to be subtle. Use action statements, with strong verbs, to encourage the reader to act. For example:

- Stop by today.

- Place your order now.

- Call today for a free consultation.

- Choose us for your business needs.

To get a feel for what makes a compelling benefit message and call-to-action, gather and study as many brochures and flyers as you can. Particularly look at examples from your competitors to understand how they see themselves, what they stress as most important, and, especially, how you can improve upon it.

step **3** **Build an eye-catching design**

Word processing and desktop publishing programs come equipped with templates to help guide you through the steps of simple and effective design. Great design is not complicated: as a rule, stick to no more than two typefaces in a given piece; use boldface, all caps, italics, and emphatic punctuation sparingly and they will have greater impact when you do use them.

To establish your visual identity, your marketing materials should all have a similar look. A consistent visual story will present a professional identity to new prospects and will be comfortingly familiar to repeat customers.

step **4** **Define your layout**

Graphic elements such as clip art, logos, and photographs should be used as more than just ornamentation. They should grab the reader's attention, add to the text, and draw the reader to your message. As always, use sparingly for better effect without confusion and clutter. Add background shading, borders, and boxes to separate or call attention to important information.

step **5** **Choose a production solution**

To impress prospects and customers and enhance your professional identity, don't skimp on the printing and paper quality. You wouldn't send a sloppily dressed salesperson to a customer's house to sell your products and services.

Likewise, your brochures and flyers are a chance to make a positive first impression.

Use your desktop printer for small mailing lists   If you have a small list, print your brochures and flyers on your own high-quality laser printer or color printer. This in-house option makes producing documents more affordable.

Go commercial for bigger jobs   If you plan to print in large quantities or want especially sharp graphics and photographs, have your brochure or flyer printed on a commercial printing press.

Consider high resolution   For the best results, your original document should be output to a high-resolution "imagesetter" instead of a laser or color printer. Commercial printers usually offer this service, which can be two or three times the resolution (measured in dots per inch) of a typical desktop printer.

One more tip: Don't forget to connect your messages and follow up   Coordinate all your marketing materials to work together for the most powerful effect. Offer a free brochure in your newsletter. List your address, phone, fax, e-mail, and web site addresses on all your printed materials.

How to Conduct Business Research on the Internet

The Internet is a doorway to a tremendous amount of information. You can access government databases, download spreadsheets, and locate thesauruses, dictionaries, quotes, books, discussion groups, and companies.

On the Internet you can find the federal government's latest ruling on tax deductions without shuffling through stacks of government periodicals in the basement of your local library. Or get the annual corporate reports of many publicly traded companies without phoning and requesting a copy sent in the mail. Once you know your way around the Internet, this type of information, and much more, can be found literally in minutes.

Conducting research via the Internet from your personal computer can save you hours of wading through microfiche at the library or paying a significant amount of money to a market research firm to survey potential customers. In addition, information is regularly updated on the Internet; in many cases, you have access to real-time data, conversations, and other sources of content and ideas.

step **1** **Understand the Internet**

In the most basic terms, the Internet (originally designed by the Department of Defense as a decentralized communications link among military sites) comprises thousands of computers connected by a common set of protocols, tools, and gateways and accessed through phone lines and modems.

What is a web site? The World Wide Web (WWW) is a set of services that run on top of the Internet that facilitate the electronic publication of information, workflow collaboration, and business application delivery. A web site holds information put there by a company, government agency, other organization, or individual. In addition to text and graphics, web sites can have sound and movies.

How do you access a web site? To get to and move around the web, you need browser software, such as Mosaic, Netscape, or Web Explorer.

What is a web address? Every web site has an address, called a uniform resource locator (URL). If you know the web address for a company or product you can type it on the address line at the top of the screen and your browser will take you directly to the web site. In web addresses, the "http://" stands for hypertext transfer protocol, which is the language that tells your software what type of site you are accessing.

step **2** **Set up an Internet account**

To get connected, you need to find an Internet service provider (ISP), such as America Online (AOL), CompuServe, Earthlink, Microsoft Network, or Prodigy, or some other conduit that offers Internet linking services, such as the telephone companies. Account charges will vary, depending on the variety of capabilities and the speed and consistency of service you require, but generally run about $20 a month plus activity charges when you're online.

step **3** **Conduct an effective search**

Once you're up and running on the Internet, your research is bounded only by your imagination. The easiest way to locate multiple sources related to a given topic is to use a search engine (an index of the content on the web), such as Alta Vista, Excite, Hotbot, Infoseek, Lycos, WebCrawler, or Yahoo.

Typing in key words, you'll soon see the results of the search. The search engine will tell you approximately how many matches met your criteria, typically displaying the first 10 or 20 matches. Find the site that interests you and click the underlined words in the entry to go directly to that web site.

To be thorough, you should repeat your search using several different search engines. Also try different ways of describing your topics, using abbreviations, acronyms, and synonyms.

step **4** **Know where to look**

You will refine your research skills with experience. To start, try entering your business type—Income Tax Accounting or Wine Producing, for example—to see what comes up. Check out the web pages of your competitors and customers.

There are thousands of sites on the web, and it is easy to get lost in cyberspace. As you discover particularly useful sites you can "bookmark" or save them for immediate access on subsequent visits. You might consider bookmarking a portfolio of sites that include those of key customers and competitors; news organizations and publications; the Small Business Administration; trade associations for your industry; and unusual sources of facts, figures, and anecdotes from which to draw for your newsletter or other marketing materials.

How to Create a Simple Web Page

Today, anyone can publish on the World Wide Web. On the web, you'll have an opportunity to get closer to your existing customers and reach a larger market. Your web site gives your customers real-time access to information about your company and its products and services, offers online ordering capabilities, and can enhance your relationships by serving as a link to other related sites. At the same time, the web allows you to stretch your own marketing resources by offering inexpensive access to customers worldwide and by establishing online alliances with suppliers, distributors, and even competitors.

step **1** **Understand the Internet**

Before you consider advertising or establishing a storefront on the World Wide Web, get out there and get familiar with what it can offer. Your access to the web will be managed through your Internet service provider. Once you set up your account and choose a browser, the world will be at your fingertips.

What is a web page?   You can think of a web site as an interactive brochure about your company. Web sites can include sound, movies, text, graphics, and hyperlinks, which allow viewers to move from one page to another by simply clicking on a word or phrase. A web page is simply what you see on the screen when you access a web document or site.

Can I reach my target audience on the web?   According to a recent survey, almost 60 percent of the people who predominantly use the web have a bachelor's degree or better. But you'll need to spend more time finding out if the people you are interested in reaching are using the Internet.

step **2** **Choose a provider**

Before creating your web pages, you'll need to decide how you are going to get your site on the web. You may choose to run your own web server or pick an Internet service provider to host your site. You may want to have the following services:

- unlimited World Wide Web browsing

- electronic mail access

- personal web pages

- newsgroup and bulletin board access

- file transfer protocol (FTP) and Gopher access

Typically, you would choose from among these three basic options:

Lease space from an ISP   For a small monthly rate, many Internet service providers will host web sites for their customers.

Hire a web publishing firm   Firms that provide assistance with web page design and maintenance often rent you space for your web site for a small fee.

Set up your own server   This requires a dedicated high-powered personal computer or workstation for web publishing and maintenance. You'll also need web server software.

step **3** Create your web site

You can establish a simple web site without any technical knowledge. Software packages are available that provide step-by-step guides and templates for automatic style options. You can import files and documents describing your company's products and services and begin to set up interactive features, such as e-mail customer registration and electronic ordering forms.

A word about security If your company is connected to the Internet, the public does not have direct or legal access to your internal data or networks through your web site.

step **4** Make your site interactive

Several basic design principles apply to web page design just as they do to print materials. Too many typefaces, colors, and graphics can clutter your pages and make them difficult to read. The best rule is to keep it simple. Large graphics and photographs can take too long for viewers to download, so keep graphics small.

There are also features unique to online publishing. Such features as hot spots, moving graphics, navigation buttons, and hyperlinks get the web page reader involved.

Add navigation buttons If your web site will include more than one page, be sure to include navigation buttons that allow viewers to quickly access your welcome page, the previous page, and the next page.

Create hyperlinks A hyperlink is an underlined or otherwise emphasized word or phrase that, when clicked with the mouse, displays another document or takes the user to another site. A good web site will offer a number of hyperlinks to allow your customers to sail through your pages directly to the information they want most.

step **5** Attract visitors to your web site

If you want to attract lots of visitors to your web site you'll need to spend some time publicizing it. Take every opportunity you can think of to promote your site.

For starters, you'll want to add your web address to all of your marketing materials, such as print ads, brochures, flyers, letterhead, and business cards, as well as to your voice mail messages.

Send notices via e-mail to Internet directories and search engines such as InfoSeek, Lycos, Webcrawler, and Yahoo. This way, when web surfers come by and type in the keyword "rugs," your rug factory's name, description, and web address (uniform resource locator, or URL) pop up.

For a fee, businesses such as Submit-It and Postmaster will submit your URL to several hundred search engines, directories, What's New listings, and more. Just type in your web site description and these services automatically do the rest.

Post notices to relevant mailing lists and Usenet newsgroups. They are a good way to spread the word about your new site. But beware: not all newsgroups and mailing lists allow advertising, so be sure to check.

Tips for Internet publishing

Conducting business online (such as advertising, accepting online credit card transactions, games, and contests) raises a large number of legal issues. Before you conduct that kind of commercial activity via your web site, be sure to consult with your lawyer.

Change your web page often   You'll find that visitors will come back to your page regularly if you offer them new and compelling information on a frequent basis. So plan weekly or monthly updates to boost traffic.

Include a feedback form in the design of your web page
Provide visitors with a way to tell you what they think, ask
questions about your products, or offer new ideas.

55 Technology Tips

The virtual office

tip **1** **Make sure there are enough computers to go around**
It's essential that there are enough tools on hand for all of your employees. It takes an investment in technology to see a return.

tip **2** **Invest in the proper tools**
Slow computers with limited memory and hard disk capacity cost you money in lost productivity. The right tools always pay for themselves.

tip **3** **Monitor software installations**
To speed upgrades, keep a log of what software is installed on each computer—including version number—when and by whom.

tip **4** **Be sure your telephone is always answered**

Even when no one's in the office, you can set up your computer with a voice mail system that can log and direct messages to the appropriate staff member.

tip **5** **Itemize your assets**

Create tracking sheets to itemize office furnishings as well as the serial numbers of computer hardware and software. With this information on hand, you can save lots of time and trouble.

tip **6** **Maintain consistent internal communications**

Establish a central mailbox to alert employees that mail or packages have arrived instead of depositing them on desks.

tip **7** **Reduce payroll expenses**

Use electronic spreadsheets to keep your payroll and tax records up to date, speeding your work and reducing outside bookkeeping and accounting expenses.

tip **8** **Run a tight ship**

Invest in financial planning software that will allow you to analyze income, cash flow, and sales data on an ongoing basis and create profit-and-loss statements to track actual versus projected income and expenses; avoid unpleasant surprises; identify new profit opportunities; and make informed purchasing, borrowing, and leasing decisions.

tip **9** **Monitor your receivables**

Use spreadsheets to prepare your invoices and track payments. This saves time, improves accuracy, and helps you identify problems and take appropriate action before it's too late.

tip 10   Simplify ordering and order fulfillment

Reduce postage costs and delays by submitting (and inviting) e-mail purchase orders and order confirmations.

tip 11   Stay on top of your stock

Keep your inventory current by entering all purchase orders electronically and automatically tracking stock in real time. Prepare your own customized invoice and packing lists.

tip 12   Send faxes directly from your computer

Don't waste time printing out paper faxes and walking across the room to place them in your fax machine. Set up your system to automatically dial the correct number and send them from your computer.

tip 13   Save money by posting "housekeeping" information electronically

Reduce printing costs and eliminate misunderstandings with customers, employees, and vendors by sharing procedural information on an intranet or password-protected web site. Post and update documents with time-sensitive information to the web automatically, with no HTML knowledge required.

Customers

tip 14 Organize customers and prospect information

Set up a database to organize customer and prospect names, addresses, phone numbers, fax numbers, and e-mail addresses in one place, making the information easy to use, reuse, share, and take with you on your travels.

tip 15 Give prospects a reason to act now

Always build immediacy into your offerings. When sending out information, always include a coupon offering special savings (or other incentives) if the customer purchases within a limited time.

tip 16 Survey your customers

Make sure you're spending your money wisely. Find out what you're doing right and what you're doing wrong. Distribute surveys by mail, in person, or on the web. Invite e-mail responses and use electronic data entry spreadsheets to input information and chart the results.

tip 17 Track the results of your advertising

Consider printing coupons on different colored paper or use special telephone extension numbers, web site addresses, and post office boxes to track how people respond to different advertising efforts. Use electronic spreadsheets to track the results.

tip 18 Become an authority in your field

Send your web address and copies of your newsletters

to the press and let them know you're available for comment. Soon you'll be quoted as an authority.

tip **19** **Give away valuable information for free**

Use newsletters and your web site to establish yourself as a knowledgeable source of information. Helping your customers and prospects make informed decisions builds confidence in you, making it easier for them to say "yes."

tip **20** **Identify buying trends**

Analyze your customer database to identify clusters of customers by their addresses, helping you target future marketing efforts.

tip **21** **Always thank your customers**

Prepare customized thank-you letters and envelopes that let your customers know you appreciate their business.

tip **22** **Place spreadsheets on the web**

This makes it easy to keep customers and prospects informed about the latest prices and current inventory. Use password-protected web sites or intranets to keep your outside sales staff up-to-date with the latest pricing and product information.

tip **23** **Invite customers to a Preferred Customers Sale**

Using mail merge capabilities, you can create and address a low-budget postcard promotion that will help you quickly generate business and reduce excess inventory.

tip 24 Give customers a reason to come back

When thanking customers for their purchase, include a self-produced coupon or gift certificate good for special savings on additional purchases made within a limited amount of time.

tip 25 Make it easy for prospects to find you

Use an electronic mapping program to show the location of your business. Insert it in your brochures, newsletters, and web site. Customize directions for individual customers by showing the best route from their location to yours.

tip 26 Investigate co-marketing opportunities

Locate businesses in your area that market to customers with similar buying habits and investigate joint mailings and promotions. You may be able to sell them space in your newsletter or catalog, or enclose their flyers with your mailings.

Time management

tip 27 Automate, don't duplicate

Use software that can help you save valuable time by: scheduling, prioritizing, and reminding you of important tasks; searching for electronic files by a variety of criteria; monitoring your use of the telephone with key customers to keep track of topics covered, for future reference.

tip 28 Run faster, more productive meetings

Keep your meetings on track by making everyone's schedule available at a glance; posting a calendar of important upcoming events or deadlines; electronically preparing and distributing meeting agendas in advance; and sharing minutes afterward.

tip 29 Record as you go

Keep daily track of travel expenses. Receipts can clog your wallet or get misplaced when you travel, so establish a daily routine to record your expenses electronically.

tip 30 Share the work

Use groupware to permit more than one person to work on a document or spreadsheet at a time, saving time and making it easy to track revisions.

tip 31 Avoid reinventing the wheel each time you send a letter or proposal

Set up templates to insert frequently used text and graphic elements into your correspondence, proposals, and reports with just a few keystrokes, saving time and reducing secretarial costs.

tip 32 Back up regularly

Establish a manageable schedule for backing up your important data and storing it safely and securely off-site.

tip 33 Keep track of your time (and your employees' time)

Create forms that enable you to prepare customized time and billing reports that show where your time goes. These reports also help you substantiate charges if you're asked. You can even automatically record how much computer time is spent on each file or activity.

tip **34** Make the most of your travel time

Electronic mapping programs help you save time and resources by locating key landmarks (such as airports, hotels, and restaurants) and determining the most efficient route to your destination. You can plot the most efficient route for a whole day's worth of meetings and print out the results.

The Internet

tip **35** Presell your competence to prospects using the World Wide Web

The web permits you to share information with prospects without incurring heavy production, printing, and postage expenses. Be sure to keep your web site up-to-date on new products, upcoming events, special promotions, and new additions to your staff.

tip **36** Promote your web site

Always include your Web address in brochures, newsletters, and broadcast advertising, and on your letterhead. Be sure to register your address with web search engines.

tip **37** Link your documents to the web

Insert web hyperlinks into reports, proposals, and sales letters you distribute electronically. This permits readers to instantly access more information that catches their attention.

tip **38** Invite comments from web site visitors

Give visitors to your web site a reason to establish a relationship with you. Ask them what they'd like to see that's not there. Encourage them to respond via e-mail. This helps you build a low-cost promotion list, fine-tune web site content, and establish comfort and familiarity.

tip **39** **Don't be a stranger**

Customers like to know who they're buying from. Introduce yourself to prospects before they meet you by scanning photographs into your brochures, newsletters, and on your web site to pave the way for successful meetings.

tip **40** **Link your web site to complementary sites**

Attract newcomers to your web site by linking it to those of firms selling products that appeal to similar buyers.

tip **41** **Use the web as a low-cost promotional medium**

By posting one-of-a-kind specials and limited-time offerings on your web site, you can generate repeat visits and eliminate deadwood from your inventory.

tip **42** **Spend more time selling, less time answering questions**

Include a feature in your web site that answers questions first-time buyers frequently ask. This establishes your credibility before you even meet the prospect, so you can make the most of your selling time.

tip **43** **Surf the Internet**

Browse the Internet periodically to stay one step ahead: check out vendor sites for price reductions and competitors' sites for new ideas.

tip 44 Invest in e-mail for everyone

For maximum productivity, every member of your staff—regardless of level or length of tenure—should be assigned an e-mail address.

tip 45 Use the Internet to recruit new employees

A good-looking, up-to-date web site can help you attract new employees. Place job openings on the web and encourage e-mail responses.

tip 46 Use e-mail to reduce mail, phone, and fax costs and eliminate telephone tag

Communicate with customers, prospects, and vendors instantaneously via e-mail without incurring postage, courier, or long-distance telephone charges.

tip 47 Use e-mail to enhance visibility

Become a contributor to electronic discussion groups that your customers and prospects frequent. Your presence and opinions will presell your expertise.

Low-cost/high-return marketing

tip 48 Become a promotion powerhouse

Get the word out at low cost by designing and producing your own flyers, special event announcements, postcards, signs, greeting cards, and point-of-purchase materials.

tip **49** **Use newsletters to keep customers informed**

Newsletters let you target your message directly to those most likely to buy from you. Create an ongoing newsletter program to introduce new products, share success stories, and keep your name in front of customers and prospects.

tip **50** **Tell your story in a brochure you create yourself**

Create your own brochure to describe your background, business philosophy, and the unique benefits prospects enjoy when they buy from you.

tip **51** **Let the press help you get the word out**

Link your database and word processing programs to prepare and address professionally formatted press releases announcing your upcoming events or important achievements to media contacts.

tip **52** **Prepare a professional information package**

Design your own custom labels for CDs, diskettes, videocassettes, and other items—even wine bottles. Quality packaging enhances the information's or product's value.

tip **53** **Project a professional identity with every piece of correspondence**

Design your own business cards, letterhead, and envelopes. Draw from your contact database to generate mailing labels quickly and accurately.

tip **54** **Investigate printing on demand**

Prepare letterheads, invoices, forms, thank-you cards, manuals, and price lists as you need them, instead of printing them in advance. This allows you to accommodate last-minute changes, reduces your overhead, and eliminates chances you'll run out or have to discard stock with outdated information.

tip 55 Always project the same identity

Always use the same typefaces, colors, layout, and paper on your print communications, including invoices, contracts, and purchase orders. Consistency builds brand recognition (i.e., familiarity) and establishes a professional identity. The same goes for all of your print and online marketing materials: ads, business cards, letterhead, brochures, newsletters, and even your web site.

What's Your Techficiency Quotient?

Are you taking full advantage of the way technology can help you organize, promote, and grow your business effectively? The following questions will help you determine your "Techficiency Quotient." How accurately do the following statements describe your business? Read the following statements and circle the most appropriate response. Then compare your responses to the comments on pages 203–204. This will help you to identify areas where technology can help you create new business, increase your profits, and work as efficiently as possible.

The quiz

1. I have to look in more than one place when dialing the phone, sending a fax, addressing an envelope, or sending e-mail to customers, prospects, or vendors.

Always   Usually   Sometimes   Never

2. I return phone calls and follow up when I promise.

Always   **Usually**   **Sometimes**   **Never**

3. I have accurate records of how much time I've spent on the phone with clients or working on their projects.

Always   **Usually**   **Sometimes**   **Never**

4. I can easily share my customer and prospect database or take it with me on trips.

Always   **Usually**   **Sometimes**   **Never**

5. I lose notes made while talking on the phone.

Always   **Usually**   **Sometimes**   **Never**

6. My staff and I struggle to meet deadlines.

Always   **Usually**   **Sometimes**   **Never**

7. Scheduling meetings is a hassle.

Always   **Usually**   **Sometimes**   **Never**

8. I'm paying less than before for telephone, postage, and courier charges.

Always   **Usually**   **Sometimes**   **Never**

9. I can provide company and product information to my customers without spending a lot of money on printing, postage, and overnight delivery services.

Always   **Usually**   **Sometimes**   **Never**

10. My staff and I spend a lot of time answering the same questions over and over again.

Always   **Usually**   **Sometimes**   **Never**

11. Prospects from out of my firm's normal marketing area search us out because of our specialized expertise.

> **Always**   **Usually**   **Sometimes**   **Never**

12. I receive unsolicited résumés from qualified job candidates.

> **Always**   **Usually**   **Sometimes**   **Never**

13. I can tell you how close current income and expenses are to projected income and expenses.

> **Always**   **Usually**   **Sometimes**   **Never**

14. I can tell you which of my products and services make the most money.

> **Always**   **Usually**   **Sometimes**   **Never**

15. Tax time is an expensive and stressful hassle.

> **Always**   **Usually**   **Sometimes**   **Never**

16. I rely on outside advice when comparing leasing and financing alternatives.

> **Always**   **Usually**   **Sometimes**   **Never**

17. I can immediately tell you the value of our computers, furnishings, and other physical assets and provide serial numbers.

> **Always**   **Usually**   **Sometimes**   **Never**

18. Customers say our location is hard to find.

> **Always**   **Usually**   **Sometimes**   **Never**

19. I get lost and am late when visiting out-of-town customers and prospects for the first time.

      Always   **Usually**   **Sometimes**   **Never**

20. I find myself retyping the same information repeatedly when preparing correspondence, e-mail, proposals, and reports.

      Always   **Usually**   **Sometimes**   **Never**

21. A lot of our business comes from repeat customers.

      Always   **Usually**   **Sometimes**   **Never**

22. Customers and prospects (and competitors) comment on the professional appearance of our brochures, newsletters, and web site.

      Always   **Usually**   **Sometimes**   **Never**

23. My firm's brochures, newsletters, postcards, and flyers share a common, distinctive look.

      Always   **Usually**   **Sometimes**   **Never**

24. Our brochures, newsletter, and web site project the image of a much larger firm.

      Always   **Usually**   **Sometimes**   **Never**

25. We pay a lot for outside graphic design and production.

      Always   **Usually**   **Sometimes**   **Never**

**How to evaluate
your techficiency quotient**

Use the comments below when evaluating your responses.

Questions 1–7
If you frequently answered "Always" or "Usually" to questions 1, 5, 6, and 7, and "Sometimes" or "Never" to questions 2–4, you're working harder than you have to. You could benefit from a software package that integrates customer and contact information, automates follow-up, and tracks your time.

Question 8
If you answered "Sometimes" or "Never," you're wasting money by not using e-mail to communicate with customers and prospects and avoid costly postage, long-distance telephone, and overnight courier charges.

Questions 9–12
If you answered "Never" or "Sometimes" to most of these questions, you're probably not taking advantage of the Internet's ability to introduce you to new customers and build closer relationships with existing prospects, customers, and prospective employees. Software kits are available for preparing and posting a web site, even if you have no previous design or Internet experience.

Questions 13–17
If you answered "Always" or "Usually" to the majority of these questions, you're probably not taking advantage of financial management software. Chances are you're paying more than you have to for outside services and working harder than necessary.

Questions 18–19
If you answered "Always" or "Usually" to these questions, a mapping program could help you save time, reduce unnecessary travel expenses, and make it easier for customers to find you.

Question 20

If you answered "Always" or "Usually" to this question, you could save time by using your word processing program to create templates, allowing you to automatically insert frequently used paragraphs and phrases.

Question 21

If you answered "Never" or "Sometimes" to this question, you're probably not taking advantage of word processing or desktop publishing programs to create personalized thank-you letters, postcards, and newsletters that maintain your visibility with past customers. Since it can cost as much as six times as much to sell to a new customer as to a past customer, you're probably working inefficiently and cutting into potential profits.

Questions 22–25

If you answered "Never" or "Sometimes" to questions 22–24 and "Always" or "Sometimes" to question 25, you're probably not enjoying the benefits of using a desktop publishing kit to help you produce your own marketing materials.

Index

AAA Internet Promotions, 107
Accounting software, 94–95
Advertising, 35, 127
A list, 53
Alta Vista, 9
Amazement, 37–38
Amazon.com, 19
Anxiety, 4–6
Appointments, 84
Attitude, 25–27
Audiovisual aids, 130

Beeper, 23
Bit Group, 104
B list, 53
Bolles, Richard, 81
Book, 131
Booklet, 131
Brochure, 3, 26, 30, 128
    computer disk, 56
    style sheet, 83
    web address on, 110
    web site, 103
Bulletin board system (BBS), 9, 114
Business card, 30, 110, 125, 127
Business plan, 25

Calendar, 25, 77–79, 122
Candor revolution, 139
Car phone, 18, 84
Catalog, 30, 110, 128
CD-ROM, 56
Cell phone, 18, 132
Charles River Strategies, 89, 93
Chat room, 103, 113, 138
Classified ads, 103, 113

Client/server network, 92
Clinics, 26
Club ID card, 129. See also ID card
Collaboration, 87–100, 142. See also
    Cooperation; Interdependence;
    Strategic alliance
Commitment, 31–39, 40, 142
Communications, 99
    changing, 12
    new infrastructures, 138
    professional-looking, 122
Competition, 26, 142
    technology use, 56, 62, 132, 148
    web-site, 105
Computer, 6, 18, 30
    as compulsory, 143
    connecting, 89
    electrical power for, 22
    Internet, networking and, 100
    laptop, 23, 84
    location of, 77
    networking, 132
    PC sales, 104
    purchasing, 65–67
    for speed and saving time, 71
    system, 125
Computer-aided design, 99
Conference, online, 113
Confidence, 33
Connectivity revolution, 138
Consciousness revolution, 138
Consistency, 32–33, 40–41
Consultations, free, 26, 52
Contact management software, 74,
    78, 82
Content, providing, 102–103

Contest entry form, 129
Cooperation, 26–27, 40, 87. *See also*
    Collaboration; Interdepen-
    dence; Strategic alliance
Copier, 18, 22
Cost
    networking, 95
    technology, 69, 143
Coupon, 51, 56, 129
Credibility, 26, 142
Customer
    business of, 43–58
    changing, 56–58
    confident, 33, 41
    contacts, 54
    existing, 37
    hotline, 56
    information about, 47–48
    intimacy with, 48
    list, 30
    new vs. existing, 45
    online commerce and, 116
    questionnaire, 45, 47
    reading habits of, 116
    relationship with, 27, 44, 46,
        49–52
    satisfaction, 48
    technology use, 56, 62
    unhappy, 52
Customer service, 140
    deterrents to, 53
    flexibility, 25–26
    information, 44–45
    outstanding, 52
    for repeat and referral business,
        46
    superstar, 56
    technology and, 24, 55
    with virtual office, 19

Daily log, 73
Database, 45, 54, 74–75, 123
    customer, 49

    patient, 49
    sharing, 98
Deadlines, 22
Delivery, free, 52
Dell Computer, 19
Demonstrations, 26
Desktop publishing software, 127
Dial-in remote networking, 99
Digital notepad, 18
Direct mail, 3, 35, 49, 59, 75, 126
Directory, 103
Discipline, 22
Downloading, 82
Downsizing, 6–7, 144
Drucker, Peter, 86

Easy-tech, 2, 4, 12, 120
Edison, Thomas, 99
Education revolution, 138
Effectiveness, 73
Efficiency, 73
80/20 principle, 53
E-mail, 18, 60, 76, 99, 103, 123
    address, 30, 36
    customers' use of, 62
    encouraging, 84
    follow-up, 27
    handling, 113
    ISDN lines for, 88
    "media alert" via, 107
    outside company, 92
    peer-to-peer network, 91
    personal, 54
    regular, 50, 63
    requests, 116
    snail mail vs., 104
Entrepreneurship, collaborative, 98
Envelope, 125–126
Ergonomics, 68–69

Fax, 3, 6
    campaign, 49

follow-up, 27
 regular, 50
Fax on demand, 74, 132
Fax machine, 30, 36, 60, 132, 138
 location of, 77
 with peer-to-peer network, 91
Fax modem, 18, 22
Files
 computer, 82
 paper, 78
 sharing, 98
Flexibility, 25, 140
Flipchart, 30, 131
Flyer, 3, 30, 75, 126
 follow-up, 27
 style sheet, 83
 web address on, 110
Focus (Ries), 55
Follow-up, 27, 34–35, 41
 for customer loyalty, 37
 e-mail, 116
 flyer, 27
 letters, 84
 for proof of involvement, 39
 reminders for, 74
 technology and, 122
 willingness to, 29–30
Forum, online, 113, 116
Franchise, 8
Fusion marketing, 26–27, 96, 109,
 122

Gallup Organization, 93
Gift certificate, 30, 128
Global commerce, 3, 69
Greeting card, 47, 129
Guerrilla marketing
 defined, 7
 online basic training, 112–117
 principles of, 31–40

Hardware, sharing, 98
High-touch networking, 97–98

Home-based business, 6, 8
 percentage of workforce, 16
 profits by, 146
 See also Home office; Virtual
 office
Home office, 3
Home workers, 147
Human behavior, 137

IDC/Link, 16, 94, 147
ID card, 125. *See also* Club ID card
Income Opportunities magazine, 146
Independent contractors, 17
Individuality, 140
Information
 Age, 122, 124
 revolution, 137
 shared, 88
 superhighway, 101. *See also*
 Internet
Innovation, 142
Installation, free, 52
Interactive kiosks, 56
Interdependence, 87, 122. *See also*
 Collaboration; Cooperation;
 Strategic alliance
Internet
 affordability of, 136
 computers, networking and, 100
 for connectivity, 138
 for data access, 124
 e-mail via, 123
 global community and, 3
 infancy of, 17, 104
 as information source, 137
 marketing and, 30, 35, 101–102
 mining treasures of, 101–118
 opportunities on, 9, 12
 for people access, 124
 for research, 76
 strategic alliances, 69
 in virtual office, 18
 for web marketing, 124

weekly surf through, 117
World Wide Web, 103, 115
  as Yellow Pages alternative, 125
Inventory management, 95
Invitation, 128
Invoice, 83, 110, 128
Involvement, 39
ISDN (integrated services digital
    network) lines, 82, 88, 94

Labels, 75, 127
Laptop computer, 23, 84
Letter
  direct mail, 59, 126
  follow-up, 27
  form, 84
  personal, 54
  regular, 50
  style sheet, 83
Letterhead, 110, 126
Link Resources, 6
Links, web site, 106, 109–110
Love revolution, 137–138
Lycos, 9

Magellan, 9
Mail, e-mail vs. snail, 104
Marketing
  fusion, 96, 109. *See also* Fusion
      marketing
  high-tech/high-return, 119–133
  Internet, 30, 35, 101–102
  investment, 32, 40
  online, 105
  small business, 29–42
  subsequent to sale, 36–37, 41
  web, 124–125
  what is? 29–30
Marketing-on-hold telephone, 74
Marketing plan, 122
  commitment to, 32
  written, 64–65

Measurement, 37–39
Modem, 6
  fax, 18, 22
  high-speed, 82, 94
  for peer-to-peer network, 91
  for telecommuting, 92
Morale, 19, 24
Multimedia presentation, 56, 125,
    131
Multitasking, 99

Net. *See* Internet
Network, 24, 56
  average small business, 92–93
  client/server, 92
  computer, 138
  peer-to-peer, 90–92
  See also Networking
Networking
  computer for, 132
  computer, Internet and, 100
  cost of, 95
  dial-in remote, 99
  examples of, 93–94
  external, 96–97
  hardware, 82
  high-touch, 97–98
  in-person, 141
  participation in, 89
  as sharing, 88–100
  similarities in small business, 89
  small business and, 94–95
  See also Network
Newsgroup, 9, 103, 111, 113, 116
Newsletter, 3–4, 26, 30, 75, 125–126
  follow-up, 27
  regular, 50
  style sheet, 83
  web address in, 110
Notepad, digital, 18

Offline, 110, 112

Online
  basic training, 112–117
  column, 124
  commerce, 116
  communication, 4
  coupons, 56
  downloading, 82
  services, 18

Pager, 138
Paperwork, 78, 84
Patience, 33–34
Payroll, 95
PDA (personal digital assistant), 18
Peer-to-peer network, 90–92
People business, 42
Personalization, 140
Phone, 18
  answering, 29
  car, 84
  hands-free, 82
  location of, 77
Phone call, 83–84
  follow-up, 27
  regular, 50
Phone log, 78
Plan
  business, 25
  marketing, 32, 64–65, 122
  next day, 79
  strategic, 142
  ten-step, 61–68
  time-saving, 72–76
Point-of-purchase materials, 130
Postcard, 126
  follow-up, 27
  regular, 50
  web address on, 110
Press release, 110, 130
Price lists, 127
Printer, 6, 18, 89, 125
Product development cycle, 141
Productivity, 19, 24

Professionalism, 142
Profitability, 24, 36, 142
Proposal, 30, 75, 131
Prospect, 37
  relationship with, 27
  visiting web site, 108–109
Psychology revolution, 137
Public relations, 35
Purchase order forms, 128

Questionnaire
  customer, 45, 47
  See also Research questionnaire

Real-time chatting, 124
Records, electronic storage of, 91
Remote access, 92
Repairs, free, 52
Research, 61–62
Research questionnaire, 3, 131. *See also* Questionnaire
Revolutions, 136–140
Ries, Al, 55

Samples, 26
Satellite transmission, 56
Scanner, 6, 125
Search engine, 103, 115
Seminars, 26
Sensitivity, 142
Shipping
  free, 51
  label, 75
Sign, 3, 30, 75, 130
Silicon Valley, 140–141
Small business
  employees in U.S., 144
  future for, 135–148
  goals of, 145
  marketing your, 29–42
  networking and, 89, 92–95
  technology as boon to, 30–31
Small Business Administration, 146

Snail mail
    e-mail vs., 104
    follow-up, 27
Software
    accounting, 94–95
    invoicing, 83
    purchasing, 68
    sharing, 98
    upgrading, 65
Spreadsheets, 91
Staff, 64–65
Stationery, 29
Strategic alliance, 69. *See also*
        Collaboration; Cooperation;
        Interdependence
Strategic planning, 142
Style sheet, 83

Tax preparation, 95
Technology
    anxiety about, 60–61
    comfort level with, 140
    competitors' use, 132, 148
    cost of, 69
    customers' use, 56, 62
    at ease with, 27
    for high returns, 123–133
    increasing pace of, 66
    investing in, 10–11, 143
    revenue and, 24
    revolution, 136
    time-saving with, 82–83
    as tool, 6
    upgrading, 69, 143
    weapons of, 3
Telecommuter, 17, 92, 146
Teleconferencing, 56
Telemarketing, 35
Telephone, 30, 138
    after hours, 51
    appointments, 83
    call, 54
    cellular, 132

    impact of, 31
    marketing-on-hold, 74
Thank-you notes, 84
3Com, 90, 93
Time
    free, 145
    guerrillas and, 72
    revolution, 136
    saving money by saving, 71–86
    tips for saving, 77–79
    well-managed, 85–86
Time bandits, 79–81
Time-saving
    plan, 72–76
    with technology, 82–83
    without technology, 83–84
Tip sheets, 51
"To do" list, 77–78
Toll-free hotline, 51
Trade show materials, 130
Trends, 142

Video conferencing, 56, 138
Virtual
    defined, 15, 139
    as state of mind, 15–17
Virtual office, 16–27
    benefits, 19
    contents, 18
    downside, 20–22
    focus, 54–55
    growth, 16–17
    truck as, 23
    See also Home-based business;
        Home office
Voice mail system, 63, 74

Web page
    as digital portfolio, 99
    e-mail response to, 30
    software to develop, 107
    See also Web site

Web site, 3, 51, 75
  address, 110, 111
  announcing, 111
  brochure, 103
  for business details, 36
  for co-marketing, 56
  as content provider, 103, 105
  customer-oriented, 47–48
  customers use of, 62
  e-mail through, 105
  launching, 108
  links, 106, 109–110
  as order fulfillment vehicle, 113
  promoting other sites, 107
  responses to, 108–109
  as session, 105
  software to create, 104
  visiting own, 116
  See also Web page
What Color Is Your Parachute?
  (Bolles), 81
Word-of-mouth marketing, 39
Word processing, 60, 91, 99
Work orders, 85
Work revolution, 139
Workweek, 147
World Wide Web, 103, 115
Writing, 26, 141

Yahoo, 9
Yellow Pages
  Internet as alternative to, 125
  web address in, 110

Continue your guerrilla training with

The Guerrilla Marketing Newsletter

Published continuously since 1986, *The Guerrilla Marketing Newsletter* provides you with state-of-the-moment insights to maximize the profits you can obtain through marketing. The newsletter is written to furnish you with the cream of the new guerrilla marketing information from around the world along with new perspectives on existing wisdom about marketing. It is filled with practical advice, the latest research, upcoming trends, and brand-new marketing techniques—all designed to pay off in profits to you.

A yearly subscription costs $59 for six issues.

All subscribers are given this unique guarantee: If you aren't convinced after examining your first issue for 30 days that the newsletter will raise your profits, your subscription fee will be refunded—along with $2 just for trying.

To subscribe, and get a free brochure, call, write, or e-mail us at:

Guerrilla Marketing International
260 Cascade Drive, P.O. Box 1336
Mill Valley, CA 94902, U.S.A.
1-800-748-6444 (in California, 415-381-8361)
E-mail: GMINTL@aol.com

If you're online, check the Guerrilla Marketing Online magazine at www.gmarketing.com.

About Microsoft's
America at Work Initiative

Microsoft's *America at Work* program is a broad-based educational initiative designed to help small business owners learn about and experience the benefits of information technology. As part of this initiative, Microsoft teamed up with small business consultant and widely published author, Jay Conrad Levinson, to establish a forum for the dynamic exchange of ideas about the ways in which technology is transforming small businesses. *Guerrilla Marketing With Technology* evolved directly from this dialogue, literally taking shape in real time, as adventurous entrepreneurs were encouraged to share questions, insights, and solutions with Jay and each other via the Microsoft Small Business web site.

The *America at Work* initiative also produced an award-winning set of videos that showcase stories of small businesses using technology to become more successful—and the steps they took to get there. In addition, Microsoft has partnered with several national business development organizations—representing such diverse fields as law, accounting, and real estate—to form the Microsoft Small Business Technology Partnership, which is committed to computer technology and the innovative ways in which it can be applied to small business issues. The Microsoft Small Business Technology Partnership Board acts as a leading technological and educational resource for American small businesses, and serves as an ongoing leadership forum for the discussion of computing solutions and opportunities presented by the Internet.

For more information on how technology can help small businesses thrive, visit the Microsoft Small Business web site, /Smallbiz, at http://www.microsoft.com/smallbiz, or call Microsoft's small business technology hot line at 1-800-60-SOURCE.